D0916517

E. Hadorn

Experimental Studies of Amphibian Development

Translated by D. Turner

With 45 Figures

Springer Verlag New York Heidelberg Berlin 1974

Professor Dr. Ernst Hadorn
Zoologisch-Vergl.
Anatomisches Institut der Universität Zürich,
Künstlergasse 16, CH-8006 Zurich

Translated from the German edition Verständliche Wissen-
schaft, Band 77, E. Hadorn „Experimentelle Entwicklungs-
forschung, im besonderen an Amphibien", 2nd enlarged
Edition

ISBN 0-387-06644-6 Springer-Verlag New York Heidelberg Berlin
ISBN 3-540-06644-6 Springer-Verlag Berlin Heidelberg New York

This work is subject to copyright. All rights are reserved, whether the whole or part of the material is
concerned, specifically those of translation, reprinting, re-use of illustrations, broadcasting, reproduction by
photocopying machine or similar means, and storage in data banks. Under § 54 of the German Copyright
Law, where copies are made for other than private use, a fee is payable to the publisher, the amount of the fee
to be determined by agreement with the publisher. © by Springer-Verlag Berlin Heidelberg 1974. Library
of Congress Catalog Card Number 74-2549. Printed in Germany.
The use of registered names, trademarks, etc. in this publication does not imply, even in the absence of a
specific statement, that such names are exempt from the relevant protective laws and regulations and therefore free for general use.
Typesetting, printing, and bookbinding: Zechnersche Buchdruckerei, Speyer.

Preface

Although this is basically a translation of the second German edition published in 1970, more recent experimental findings have, in several instances, been incorporated into the text. Furthermore, we have tried to explain some of the experiments, and their possible interpretations, in a more precise way. I am very grateful to Dr. David Turner; in addition to translating the text, he was able, thanks to his experience in developmental biology, to suggest a number of improvements in the course of our collaborative discussions.

Zurich, Spring 1974   ERNST HADORN

Preface to the Second German Edition

The guiding principle of the first edition remains in force. That is, the methods and results of developmental research are introduced wherever possible with the aid of experiments on amphibians.

However, the scope of the material has been substantially expanded in newly introduced chapters on the migrations and affinities of somatic and germ cells as well as on the action of genetic factors in early development. These are fields of study which are at the center of today's research. In addition, numerous new findings have been incorporated into the text.

The author hopes that this little book will continue to facilitate understanding of exciting research problems, for the interested layman as well as for the teacher and student of biology.

It was decided to omit literature citations once again. The reader can find access to the specialized literature in the textbooks of developmental biology listed at the end of the book. References to the papers of those authors whose names appear in the figure legends can also be found in these works. To my colleagues P. S. Chen and P. Tardent, my heartfelt thanks for their helpful counsel.

Zurich, Summer 1970   ERNST HADORN

Preface to the First German Edition

Our goal in this presentation is to introduce the reader to experimental research on development. The discussion will be limited almost exclusively to investigations carried out on the eggs, embryos and larvae of the Amphibia. Other forms of life, such as sea urchins, molluscs, worms, insects and birds, have, of course, furnished vital insights into the fundamental principles and regularities of the processes of development. Yet within the framework of a small book it would be impossible to introduce the characteristics of a number of different developing systems in sufficient detail that the decisive experiments would be readily comprehensible. We are, moreover, particularly justified in restricting ourselves to the Amphibia. For some eighty years now, in many laboratories the world over, the embryos of these animals have been worked on with unflagging enthusiasm. These efforts have led to numerous fundamental discoveries that have validity far beyond the world of the Amphibia; indeed, they apply to our own human developmental processes as well. Accordingly, experiments on amphibians have long stood—and still stand today—at the center of research into the problems of development.

Of the vast wealth of experience from work on Amphibia we have selected only a small and quite arbitrarily chosen sample. Some of the most famous classical experiments are presented, but so are many which are less well known. And, by presenting some of the most recent experiments, we hope to lead the reader to the forefront of today's research. We want him to experience for himself how many are the secrets of life that remain unsolved and how each new thrust forward discloses exciting new problems.

Very many researchers have contributed to the results described in this book; only a few of them are mentioned by name. A proper citation of sources would have overburdened our text. So I ask forebearance of all those unnamed colleagues from whose work I was able to glean new knowledge. The authors of the material depicted in the figures are, however, indicated in the lengends. For the artistic execution of the figures I owe sincere thanks to my co-worker, Miss Maria Gandolla.

Zurich, Spring 1961   ERNST HADORN

Contents

Egg Laying and Provision for Posterity

As early as the end of February or the beginning of March, we can find the first egg masses (Fig. 1a) of the common European frog *(Rana temporaria)* in ponds and in the calmer waters near the shores of lakes. A little later, the common toads *(Bufo bufo)* deposit their eggs, embedded like pearls in long strings of jelly (Fig. 1b). The European newts *(Triturus* species) provide for each egg individually. They grasp leaves and stalks of aquatic plants with their hind legs and fold them around the egg as it is laid.

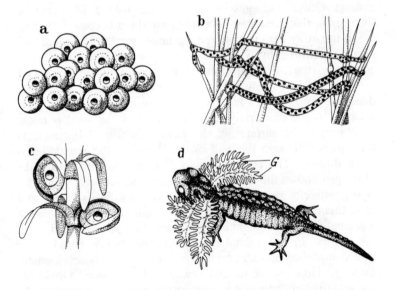

Fig. 1a—d. a Part of the egg mass of the common European frog. b Strings of toad eggs stretched between plant stems. c Two newt eggs under leaves of a water plant. d Larva removed from the oviduct of an alpine salamander, showing the extreme development of the gills (*G*)

The outermost egg coat sticks to the inner surface of the folded leaf, forming a concealed sanctuary for the development of egg and embryo (Fig. 1 c). By contrast, European salamanders retain the fertilized egg within the body of the mother. Only when early development is complete and the larvae are ready for hatching does the black-and-yellow spotted European (or "Fire") Salamander *(Salamandra salamandra)* seek an appropriate place in the brook to set free as many as fifty offspring.

For the black alpine salamander *(Salamandra atra)* development within the body of the mother actually requires some two to three years. And what goes on during this time is highly astonishing. First, each ovary releases into the oviduct anywhere from 30 to more than 100 eggs (see Fig. 2), depending on the habitat (elevation) and the age of the female. Of these germ cells, only one in each oviduct develops into an embryo and then into a larva. The egg cells (oocytes) which receive this special privilege are the ones which happen to be nearest to the cloaca in each oviduct. Only these eggs become covered with a jelly coat of the normal thickness, and as a rule only these become fertilized. All of the other eggs usually remain unfertilized, and should one become fertilized by way of exception, it will only manage to get through the earliest developmental stages. While the two lowest embryos are developing further, the rest of the oocytes unselfishly degenerate, providing a kind of nutrient broth which is gradually used up by the two privileged larvae. Part of this food is taken up throught the surfaces of the giant gills (Fig. 1d), much as food passes through the wall of the intestine; the remainder is eaten directly. The enormous gills also function in the uptake of oxygen and in the resorption of oviduct secretions.

It is possible to remove such larvae by "Caesarian section" and raise them in a glass dish. If a small worm is presented to such a prematurely born animal, it is instantly snapped up and swallowed, that is, the animal does something which could never be accomplished under normal circumstances at this developmental stage. How are we to understand such behavior? Obviously the inherited coordinated movements which are involved in the feeding act of free-living larvae have not been impaired in the course of those phylogenetic changes which have led to the evolution of the alpine salamander. When removed from its mother's body, this creature still acts, millenia later, just like the offspring of its egg-laying predecessors. The metamorphosis of the larva, too, proceeds in the unborn alpine salamander just as it does in the externally developing larvae of other amphibians (p. 122). The gills are resorbed at the proper time and the skin is reconstructed for life on land. And when the metamorphosed offspring are finally set free, their lungs are already functional. Thus during its development—and this is unusual for an amphibian—the alpine salamander need at no stage live in the water. One can consider this emancipation as an adaptation to life in high mountains, where the ponds become ice-free only during a few months and where amphibian larvae are endangered by frost even on some summer nights.

The continuing existence of an animal species is ensured if at least two offspring capable of reproduction have reached maturity by the time each pair of parents dies. The viviparous alpine salamander has reached this goal by producing only two offspring, and then only after an unusually long gestation period (p. 2). The female of the European water frog, on the other hand, lays up to 10,000 eggs every spring, and yet we do not have to fear an Egyptian plague of frogs. Murder and mayhem claim the lives of almost all the young, as embryos, as larvae or as young frogs, so that in the end only the parent generation is replaced. Throughout the animal kingdom, as parental care becomes better developed, there is an obvious decrease in the production of eggs, larvae and young animals. We can find ample confirmation of this rule of nature in the rich variety of reproductive customs among the Amphibia. The free-laying common toad deposits several thousand eggs per season, while the midwife toad (Alytes obstetricans) manages with strings of about 100 eggs, which the male winds around his hind legs and then carries around and cares for until the larvae hatch. Many thousands of individuals derived from a single mother begin their development together in frog egg masses lying in the open, whereas only a few hundred eggs are laid each spring by female newts that hide their eggs. Finally, the two viviparous salamanders show that when increasingly advanced stages of development are reached while still within the protective body of the mother, the number of offspring can decrease even further.

A Hormone as Trigger of Egg Laying

Why do frogs and newts spawn only in the spring? In these animals, as in all vertebrates, there is a small organ, called the hypophysis (Hy), or pituitary, on the underside of the brain (B) (cf. Fig. 2). This gland releases hormones into the blood in response to signals received from the hypothalamus, that part of the brain immediately adjacent. By mechanisms that are still quite obscure, seasonal changes in the environment are perceived and processed by the brain, and ultimately trigger the hypothalamus to signal the hypophysis, causing it secrete certain hormones. Thus, as the days become longer and warmer with the approach of spring, the hypophysis pours forth a specific hormone (gonadotropin, G) into the blood stream, which then acts upon the gonads of the sexually mature amphibian, promoting release of either the eggs from the ovaries (O) or the sperm from the testes (T). So-called "gonadotropic hormone" is now available in concentrated form from industrial sources. If one injects an appropriate amount of this agent under the skin of a newt or frog, the animal will promptly (within 2—3 days) release all the ripe eggs in its ovary. But one can also show directly that the hypophysis, and, more specifically, its anterior lobe, actually does produce such a hormone. One dissects out the anterior hypophyseal lobes (each one the size of a pin head) from two or three frogs and, then, taking a test animal, inserts them anywhere in one of the lymph sacs which lie between the skin and musculature of amphibians. For a short time thereafter the concentration of gonadotropic hormone becomes so high that ovulation is rapidly initiated.

Surprisingly, it is not only in springtime that this experiment is successful. In autumn, too, and throughout the whole winter, spawning of newts and frogs can be induced with gonadotropin. Supplemental hormone stimulation fails only in early summer, when the animals that have spawned in spring still have no new ripe eggs ready in their ovaries. New eggs soon mature within the emptied gonad, however, and by autumn it is packed full once again. Under natural conditions, of course, the new eggs would have to wait until the following spring before being released, for only then does the hypophysis become so active that its hormone exceeds the decisive threshold level.

4

The possibility of obtaining amphibian eggs outside of the normal spawning times is being eagerly exploited by today's experimenters. Those species which respond during the whole year are especially favored. The axolotl *(Ambystoma mexicanum)* and the South African clawed frog *(Xenopus laevis)*, among others, have really become domesticated animals in the service of developmental researchers.

Hormone dependent triggering of ovulation has found an interesting application in medical diagnosis. As one element of the profound hormonal changes which occur shortly after conception, pregnant women eliminate large amounts of a gonadotropic substance in their urine. This substance acts upon the frog ovary in the same way as the gonadotropin furnished by the hypophysis at the time of spawning. If a physician wants to know if a patient is pregnant, he injects some of her urine into a clawed frog (*Xenopus* test). If the test animal ovulates within 12—24 hours, it is proof of pregnancy. The question can be answered even more quickly using a male toad. The urine of pregnant women will trigger

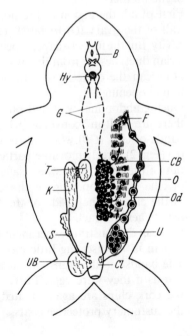

Fig. 2. Diagram of hypophysis action and migration of the gametes in the frog. The male situation is shown on the left, that for the female on the right. *B* brain; *Hy* hypophysis; *G* gonadotropic hormone; *T* testis; *K* kidney; *S* sperm duct; *UB* urinary bladder; *F* funnel; *CB* ciliary bands; *O* ovary; *Od* oviduct; *U* uterus; *Cl* cloaca

sperm release from the testes (*T*) (Fig. 2). The sperm pass through the sperm duct (*S*) into the cloaca (*Cl*) and from there also reach the urinary bladder (*UB*). A sample of toad urine can be easily collected with a pipette and examined for the presence of sperm. Swimming sperm can be observed within several hours of treatment with the urine of a pregnant woman, whereas treatment with urine from a non-gravid woman causes no release of spermatozoa.

The Egg Underway

The sperm of Amphibia find their way relatively easily to the outside. First, fine tubules connected directly to the testes (*T*) (Fig. 2) lead through a part of the kidney reserved for the passage of sperm. Then the sperm duct (*S* = Wolffian duct) takes the sperm and leads them to the cloaca (*Cl*) and urinary bladder (*UB*) whence they can reach the outside. The eggs, in comparison, must complete a much more eventful and obstacle-ridden course within the body of the mother.

First of all, the action of the hormone gonadotropin causes the wall of the ovary (*O*) to burst, releasing the eggs into the body cavity. But the funnel-shaped opening (*F*) of the oviduct (*Od* = Müllerian duct) lies far from the ovary, up in the region of the armpit. How can the quite heavy and immobile eggs find this faraway funnel opening?

On the abdominal wall and on the surface of individual organs there are built-in "conveyor belts". They are comprised of dense bands of cilia (*CB*) which all beat in the direction of the funnel (*F*) (Fig. 2). Freely movable particles, including the eggs tumbling out of the ovary, are swept safely and surely along these strips of cilia to the opening of the oviduct, where the undulations of the cilia on the inside of the funnel propel the eggs into the female genital tract.

One can demonstrate experimentally how reliable this conveyance system is, by inserting little pieces of cork into the body cavity. The bands of cilia transport such foreign bodies to the funnels, just as if they were eggs. Furthermore, once inside the oviduct, the cork chips are again treated like eggs and are wrapped in the customary protective coats.

The formation of egg coverings is among the important responsibilities of the oviduct. This will be described first for the more familiar case of the bird's egg. The giant egg cell, which we know as the egg yolk, enlarges within the ovary during some 6—7 days. The material for the tremendous cell growth is furnished by the blood stream, which transports highly specific yolk proteins from the liver where they are synthesized under the influence of female sex hormones. As it leaves the ovary, the egg cell is surrounded by the delicate vitelline membrane. This primary egg coat, elaborated by the egg cell itself, is its only covering as the egg cell enters the oviduct. Immediately after its entrance into the oviduct the egg cell becomes fertilized by the sperm which have found their way from the cloaca to this location. In the course of some twenty-four hours the fertilized bird's egg travels slowly toward the outside, and during this time it becomes enveloped by additional covering layers.

Near the top of the oviduct special glands secrete the massive protein coats (egg whites), then the tough, fibrous, shell membrane is formed. Finally, the lowest, glandular, part of the oviduct provides the material for calcifying the shell, which at this stage also gets the coloration typical for its species or strain. Uniform mixing of colored substances with the chalky secretion leads to the uniform yellow, brown, green or blue background tones. Spots, blazes and stripes are then pressed onto the egg shell. Pigments emerge at specific locations along the oviduct, and the oviduct wall functions like a stamp pad. And with the egg also rotating as it passes through, all sorts of bizarre patterns can result. The pigments involved, incidentally, are derivatives of the bile pigments that form in the liver as the result of the degradation of the red substance in blood, hemoglobin.

In Amphibia, the yolk material supplied to the enlarging egg has the same origin as in birds. And here, too, the egg cell first forms a thin primary membrane, the vitelline membrane, and then, in the oviduct (*Od*) (Fig. 2), receives additional surrounding layers. But in contrast to the bird's egg these coverings are laid down before fertilization (p. 11). These envelopes include the jelly coats, which swell rapidly once in water, so that the spawned eggs of the frog come to exceed the size of the egg-laying female several times over. As shown in Fig. 4, the newt egg is covered

7

first by two jelly coats (*JC*) and then by an adhesive coat (*AC*). Whereas in birds the egg white serves to nourish the embryo, the amphibian jelly coats have a protective function only. In the case of frogs the swelling of the coats has the additional effect of separating the eggs within the egg mass so far from one another that each is suspended freely and there is less tendency for one egg to shade another. Thus all enjoy equally the warmth of the spring sun, and a whole sibling population develops at the same tempo.

For the experimenter who would like to operate on the egg or embryo, however, the coats added in the oviduct are likely to be a nuisance. He must remove them with fine instruments or else carefully dissolve them away with certain chemicals (e.g. sodium thioglycolate). Subsequent development of the embryo is in no way impaired by such treatments.

But what about the larva which has developed to the point of hatching under natural circumstances? How does it manage to free itself from its confining coats? Here comparison to the chick cannot help us. The robust chick, having grown to fill the whole volume of its shell, files a hole in the shell with the help of the "egg tooth" on top of its beak and then forcefully cracks it open. Newts and frogs take care of this business with the help of chemistry. By the end of embryonic development the yolk reserves have been largely used up. The time has come for the larva to seek its own food. Differentiation has proceeded so far that, even in the natural habitat, the larva can dispense with further protection by the egg coats. Certain glands of the larval skin now release an enzyme which largely digests away the coats, and the larva swims free.

Fertilization of the Egg

Nature uses varied means to bring egg cells and sperm cells together. Sea urchins and many other marine animals release into the water such an enormous number of gametes that random chance alone suffices to bring about the necessary encounter. The eggs do release into the surrounding water special substances (fertilizins) which affect the sperm, changing their surfaces in a way which enables them to penetrate the egg. But no one has been able to demonstrate that these egg substances directly attract the sperm. Indeed, within the animal kingdom such a chemotaxis (p. 104) has been proved only in the case of the marine hydroid *Campanularia*.

Other animals with external fertilization, including the frogs and toads, increase the probability of egg-sperm encounters by spreading the sperm directly over the eggs as they emerge from the female's cloaca. At mating time the ardent male embraces his partner and is carried about by her for days. This "clasping reflex", which is triggered by male sex hormones, is so powerful that the male can be separated from the female only by force. In fact, a male candidate, on failing to find a female, often clings with stubborn fervor to a piece of wood or to whatever other object presents itself.

The matrimonial behavior of the newts appears to be quite complicated. At mating time, in April, the sexually mature animals travel to their spawning waters. The males, especially, acquire under the influence of sex hormones a splendid, boldly colored, raiment, and in the case of the crested newt and smooth newt the combs along the back reach their maximal size. Mating play begins when one of these males meets a female (Fig. 3a). The male places himself in front of his partner, curves his tail around toward the front and whips it back and forth so that a stream of water plays across the nose of the female. In this way, the male scents, important as triggers of the female mating performance, reach the female.

At this stage a sperm package (spermatophore, *S*) is eased out of the male's cloaca and remains attached by means of a complicated carrier (*C*) at the mating site (Fig. 3c). The carrier, with its peculiar ribs and folds, is formed in the cloaca by a sort of casting process. A liquid pours into the mold (the cloaca) and then hardens, producing a structure which reflects the intricacies of the interior walls of the cloaca. The female crawls over the sperm package (*S*) (Fig. 3b), clasps it with her lip-like cloacal margins and draws it into the interior of her cloaca (*Cl*) (Fig. 3c). In the wall of the cloaca, there is a cluster of tiny tubules (sperm pockets, *SP*, Fig. 3e) where the sperm can lodge and lie in wait like highwaymen for the ripe eggs which must pass

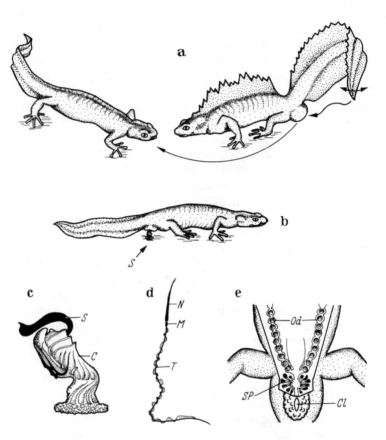

Fig. 3a—e. a Mating play of a pair of crested newts (*Triturus cristatus*; *left:* female; *right:* male). The arrows indicate how male scent is fanned toward the female. b Female grasps the sperm package or spermatophore (*S*) with her cloacal lips. c Carrier (*C*) and spermatophore (*S*) of the smooth newt (*Triturus taeniatus*). d Sperm cell of a newt, with head (*N* =cell nucleus), midpiece (*M*) and tail (*T*). e Location of the sperm pockets (*SP*) in the cloacal wall (*Cl*) of a newt; in the oviduct (*Od*) uninseminated eggs are ready for laying. (a—c after R. Hesse)

by on their way from the oviduct to the outside. As each egg passes it is dabbed with a droplet of sperm, ensuring its successful insemination. The sperm from a single supply will last for several weeks, fertilizing the one to two dozen eggs which are laid each day.

Let us now look more closely at a freshly laid alpine newt egg (Fig. 4a). The first thing we notice is that, within the rapidly swelling jelly coats, the egg cell is oriented so that the dark brown hemisphere is always facing upward while the lightly colored, yellowish-white, heavier half always faces downward. The center of the pigmented hemisphere has been designated as the "animal pole" (*an*); this point determines the egg axis which runs through the egg to the "vegetal pole" (*veg*) at the very bottom. A clear area always appears at the animal pole, and in the middle of this area (*O*) one can perceive a small pigment clump in the egg cortex which might be called the "orientation spot". This spot directs out attention to a process of fundamental importance which occurs in the oocytes of all multicellular animals.

As the nucleus of an oocyte reaches its maximal size, it has, like all other cells of the body, a double set of chromosomes. Most newt species have two times twelve chromosomes, while humans have two times twenty-three. Before the egg can become fertilizable, this "diploid" chromosome number must be reduced to one half the previous value (cf. Fig. 34, p. 94 and p. 24). This is brought about by two special nuclear divisions, which are called maturation divisions (*M I* and *M II*). In the newt, *M I* proceeds while the egg is still in the ovary. This nuclear division is accompanied by an unequal division of the ooplasm, whereby one daughter cell gets almost all of the egg material, and the other only a tiny fraction. The disadvantaged one is then ejected as the *first polar body* (*P I*) (Fig. 4b) and takes no part in what follows.

A second polar body (*P II*) (Fig. 4c) is given off in the second maturation division (*M II*). At the time of sperm penetration the newt oocyte is still in the middle of this second maturation division, with the spindle-shaped nuclear division apparatus directly under the already mentioned orientation spot. We will see later (p. 20) that the exposed position of the chromosomes enables the experimenter to remove them surgically, thus depriving the amphibian egg of its maternal chromosomes.

But now let us follow the processes of sperm penetration and fertilization more closely. In this, the newt egg does the observer an extraordinary favor. At the point where a sperm has penetrated, a distinct pigment spot in the egg cortex appears within just

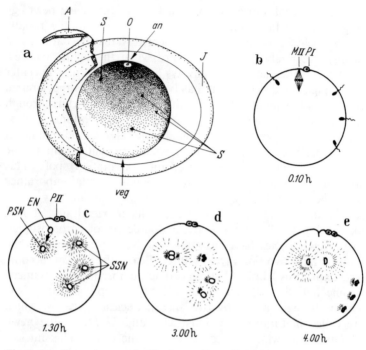

Fig. 4a—e. Stages in newt fertilization. a Egg cell, enclosed in jelly coats (*J*) and adhesive coat (*A*), just after sperm penetration; *an* animal pole, *veg* vegetal pole, *O* orientation spot, *S* four sites of sperm penetration. b A few minutes after sperm penetration (0.1 hours): *M II* second maturation division; *P I* first polar body. c After 1.3 hours: release of second polar body (*P II*); *EN* egg nucleus; *PSN* principal sperm nucleus; *SSN* supernumerary sperm nuclei. d After 3 hours: completion of fertilization. e After 4 hours: beginning of the first cleavage division and degeneration of the supernumerary sperm nuclei. (b—d after G. Fankhauser)

a few minutes. Surprisingly, we usually find evidence of multiple sperm penetration (Fig. 4a), often a half dozen or more spots. We ask if there isn't a dangerous abnormality here; we know in fact that in sea urchins and many other animals subsequent development miscarries when more than one sperm penetrates. Such *polyspermy* is, however, physiological (i. e. normal) for newts. In order to understand how normal development is possible despite polyspermy, we will have to trace out the fate of each sperm nucleus.

Each sperm is comprised of head, midpiece and tail (Fig. 3 d). The tail part, as organ of motility, has fulfilled its task as soon as the oocyte has been reached. We need therefore only consider the roles of head and midpiece. Let us take the case (Fig. 4) of an egg which has been penetrated by four sperm. At first, all contestants behave identically. Each sperm head swells somewhat and thereby reveals its true nature as a cell nucleus. The midpiece releases a "centrosome" about which the star shaped aster is organized (Fig. 4c). Now the egg nucleus (*EN*, arrow) begins to move toward whichever sperm nucleus lies closest to it. This "chosen one" can now fuse with the egg nucleus to complete the fertilization process (Fig. 4 d). The inherited factors which will determine the direction of development and the fate of the newly founded individual are thus united in the zygote nucleus. The two haploid nuclei from egg and sperm, which in newts each contain twelve chromosomes, come together to form the diploid nucleus with its twenty-four chromosomes. All of the millions of cell nuclei of the developing organism are descendants of this first zygote nucleus. In the newt, nuclear division begins four hours after fertilization. In Fig. 4e we can see that the diploid nucleus has already divided, and that a cleavage furrow originating at the animal pole begins to divide the egg cytoplasm as well. Later on, we will follow the progression of this and subsequent cleavage divisions (Fig. 11, p. 37).

The ordered and equal distribution of the chromosomes is insured by the "spindle apparatus". Here we see the importance of the centrosome which is brought along by each sperm in its midpiece: prior to each nuclear division this organelle divides, the two daughter centrosomes move apart from one another, and the spindle apparatus is then organized between them (Fig. 4 d and e).

But whatever happened to the additional sperm? At first these supernumerary sperm nuclei (*SSN*) undergo the same changes as the successful principal sperm nucleus (*PSN*): their centrosomes are also surrounded by an aster (*SSN*). Then, however, an inhibitory substance begins to spread from the successfully fused pair of nuclei. This not only prevents the other nuclei from taking further part in development but also causes their chromosomes to clump together and degenerate. As shown in Fig. 4 d, the sperm nucleus nearest to the zygote nucleus source is the first to be affected; after another hour or so (Fig. 4e), the other contestants have been taken care of. The remains of the supernumerary sperm nuclei eventually disappear.

Fatherless and Motherless Beings

In the year 1910 the French zoologist A. Bataillon was induced by his researcher's curiosity to prick unfertilized frog eggs with a metal needle. Thus stimulated, the eggs developed into normal tadpoles and a few of them actually developed into complete little frogs. An experimental "virgin birth" or *parthenogenesis* of this sort proves that the egg cell by itself has the potential for complete development. This need not astound us all that much, for we know that the haploid maternal chromosomal set of the egg nucleus contains a complete assortment of genetic factors. That which normally is provided by the father merely leads to a doubling of the genes, and so should be dispensable.

Parthenogenesis occurs in all the major groups of animals, and has become the natural means of reproduction in many cases. The walking stick insects, for example, as well as certain weevils and moths, require no males at all. And even where insemination and fertilization do take place under normal conditions, a great variety of stimuli, such as chemicals, temperature shock, electrical or mechanical intervention, can set development in motion in the absence of sperm. The egg is primed, ready to begin development—it needs only some activating trigger, and in this the father can be replaced by artificial intervention.

Even mammalian eggs will begin their development rather readily in the absence of fertilization if they are removed from the oviduct and somehow shocked. To get further development, of course, one would have to reimplant the egg in the uterus of the same or another animal—fertilized mammalian eggs can complete development only within the mother's womb. Such an experiment is obviously much more difficult than the simple pricking of a frog egg. In only one case so far, involving birth of fatherless rabbits, has a successful outcome been reported. Despite many attempts, complete parthenogenesis of a mammal has never again been achieved. On the other hand, it is well established that in any large number of unfertilized turkey eggs, there will always be a few which will begin developing spontaneously. These fatherless creatures often develop as males as far as the more advanced embryonic stages. A few parthenogenetic turkeys have even become sexually mature, making it possible to breed them. Parthenogenesis as the normal means of reproduction has, moreover, been found in certain lizards from the Caucasus region of the Soviet Union. No males exist in these populations.

While parthenogenesis remains as a possibility everywhere, males are still involved in reproducing the great majority of living forms. Evidently there must be important factors working against a general discarding of the male sex, otherwise it would be inconceivable that nature would retain the luxury of bisexuality. In bisexual organisms, every individual is equipped with a newly assembled set of genetic material. With bisexuality various gene combinations can be tested for their adaptive value. An almost unlimited multiplicity of possible assortments is made available to natural selection. Nature is constantly experimenting with these, leading to the "breeding" of adaptive forms, and thus to those magnificent transformations which have been accomplished in the evolutionary history of living things. Are motherless organisms also possible? Is there a male counterpart to parthenogenesis, in which development proceeds from the sperm cell alone? Now of course we really can't ask too much of a sperm cell. While it contains, as we saw, just as many of the same kinds of chromosomes and genes as the egg cell, the male germ cell lacks the large body of cytoplasm which, in the egg, contains all of the machinery and energy sources so necessary for constructing the embryo. If what we want is a functioning developmental system, the naked sperm will have to have access to the cellular building blocks located in the ooplasm. And provided such "auxiliary" ooplasm is devoid of the maternal egg nucleus, any organism that develops will be truly motherless with respect to the chromosomally located genetic factors.

By the end of the last century, great classical biologists were able to realize an experimental system of this sort. By shaking inseminated sea urchin eggs, the German zoologist Theodor Boveri was able to cause them to break into fragments. Among the fragments he found pieces which contained, along with a portion of the ooplasm, only a sperm nucleus. And these actually developed—without the genetic material of the maternal nucleus—into normal sea urchin larvae. Organisms, like these of Boveri, which result from a part *(meros)* of the egg are called *merogones*.

Newt eggs provide particularly attractive possibilities for the initiation of merogonic development, since each egg is fertilized by several sperm (p. 12, Fig. 4). The experimental approach taken by Hans Spemann (Freiburg, Germany) and above all by Fritz Baltzer and his coworkers (Bern, Switzerland) is described in Fig. 5. The freshly laid egg of the smooth newt *(Triturus taeniatus)* or of the palmate newt (*Triturus helveticus*, see Fig. 7) is constricted by tightening a loop of fine child's hair. Only one of the egg

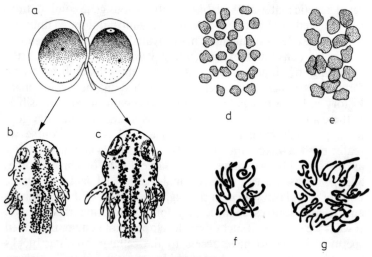

Fig. 5a—g. a Production of a newt merogone by constriction of a newly fertilized egg; *left:* merogonic half with one site of sperm penetration; *right:* diploid half with both egg nucleus (light spot) and sperm nucleus (single site of sperm penetration). b Haploid merogonic larva with many small pigment cells. c Diploid sister larva with fewer, but larger, pigment cells. d Size and density of cell nuclei in the epidermis of a haploid larva. e Corresponding region of a diploid larva. f Nuclear division of the haploid merogone showing 12 chromosomes. g The 24 chromosomes of the diploid larva. (b—e after G. Fankhauser; f and g after E. Hadorn)

halves will contain the maternal cell nucleus, while both halves receive one or more sperm nuclei. The side containing the egg nucleus develops into a normal diploid animal (c) in which the nucleus of each cell contains 12 maternal and 12 paternal chromosomes (g). This capacity, astonishing in its own right, of half an egg to produce a complete individual, is an example of *regulative development* and will be the subject of discussion at a later point (p. 59). Now, however, we are concerned with the fate of the other half, the one which received only paternal chromosomes. It produces a "motherless", haploid merogone (b) with 12 chromosomes per nucleus (f). It is also possible to produce amphibian merogones by sucking out the egg nucleus (*EN*), located near the surface of the egg (Fig. 4a), with a micropipette (Fig. 7a). This is of particular importance for those Amphibia in which the egg cannot be halved with a fine loop.

In the newt, haploid larvae can be distinguished from diploid larvae without counting the chromosomes. Because the cell size increases in direct proportion to the chromosome number, we find much smaller pigment cells (Fig. 5b) in haploid than in diploid larvae (c). The haploid organism makes up for the small cell size by doubling the number of cells, so that in the skin of a haploid animal (Fig. 5b) we observe appreciably more pigment cells than we find in the diploid larva (c). The difference between haploid and diploid is also very clear-cut in the number and size of the cell nuclei which populate the epidermis of the larval fin margin (Fig. 5d and e). Of course, the chromosome count provides direct proof of merogonic development (Fig. 5f and g). Although there is great variation in the extent of development achieved by merogones, the great majority of them cease development at an early larval stage. These haploid larvae are characterized by a number of pathological features (Fig. 6a). They typically have blunt heads, small eyes, and poorly developed gills; they also generally suffer from an incurable dropsy and have great trouble getting their circulation systems going properly.

Why most of the haploid newt merogones stop developing as early larvae, and why they are then seized by a mortal crisis, is difficult indeed to understand. Perhaps, one might think, substances indispensable for further development are synthesized in insufficient quantities. But then how to explain the variability

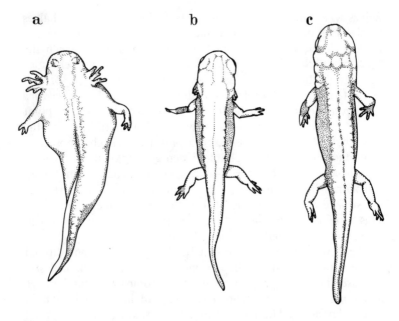

Fig. 6a—c. Abnormal development (a) of a typical haploid newt larva. b Best possible performance for a metamorphosed haploid merogone. c For comparison, a normal diploid newt after metamorphosis. The young newts (b and c) are drawn to the same scale; relative to them the larva (a) is shown somewhat enlarged. (b and c after G. Fankhauser; a after E. Hadorn)

in the length of survival, and, above all, how to explain the astounding fact that some few individuals survive the critical phase, learn to feed, and reach the latest larval stages? One merogone actually lived for 100 days at the Zoological Institute of the University of Bern (Fig. 6b); he died only after having completed the transformation (metamorphosis) to the terrestrial adult form. At the time of his death, this fellow could have claimed the world title for Oldest Living Haploid Vertebrate. And even if this record setter was stupid and sluggish in his behavior, and even if he did meet his death by drowning (something which should never happen to a metamorphosed newt), by getting as far as he did he proved that a paternal chromosome set is enough to guarantee complete development. And this in turn proves the *equivalence of paternal and maternal hereditary material* by providing a counterpart to successful parthenogenesis.

What remains unexplained is the large and disturbing degree of variability to be found in newt merogones. At least a part of this developmental variability can probably be attributed to the fact that all unfavorable genes can, potentially at least, be expressed when the chromosome set is haploid. We all carry a "genetic load" of recessive lethal and subvital factors. Such factors are normally not damaging—only in those (happily rare) cases when by chance the same recessive gene occurs in the chromosomes of both sperm and egg, resulting in a "homozygous" condition for the unfavorable gene. Far more frequently, an unfavorable gene, if present, is represented only in single dose, and is not damaging because of the presence of a "dominant" normal gene, or allele, in the corresponding position on the other chromosome of the pair. The protection afforded by the dominant effect of normal alleles is lacking in haploid merogones, and since haploid chromosome sets are going to differ from one another with respect to genes which threaten vital functions, both the extent and the direction of gene-dependent development in merogonic individuals can be expected to vary, also. We might therefore expect that only in exceptional cases, such as our "hundred day wonder" (Fig. 6b), will a merogone have genetic equipment which can satisfy, to some extent at least, the stringent requirements of the normal developmental program. Merogones probably also fail, however, for reasons other than exposure of lethal factors. Haploidy itself seems to lessen viability for reasons that are not known.

Does the Nucleus Have a Monopoly on Inheritance?

Today we know for certain that the Mendelian heritable factors (genes) are localized in the chromosomes of the cell nucleus. And yet we also know that the nucleus cannot function by itself, but only in cooperation with the cytoplasm. The question which now poses itself is: can we locate the boundaries of the nuclear and cytoplasmic spheres of influence? Theodor Boveri designed an experiment which he believed must provide the answer. He combined merogone formation with interspecific hybridization: eggs of one sea urchin species were inseminated by sperm of another species. Having first fragmented the eggs by shaking them (p. 15), Boveri was able to follow the development of egg pieces containing only paternal nuclear material. Would such hybrid merogones resemble the maternal species which supplied the cytoplasm or the paternal species which provided the nucleus?

The story of these experiments has been a long and notorious tale of woe. At first Boveri believed his sea urchin merogones to be "organisms without maternal properties", and, as such, proof for a nuclear monopoly of inherited tendencies. Thirty years later, in a masterful work which appeared only after his death, Boveri uncovered sources of error in his earlier work. He showed that his sea urchin merogones could not deliver an answer to the crucial question because they do not develop far enough. They die at early embryonic stages, at a time when none of the characteristics have yet appeared which would permit unambiguous distinction between the nucleus-donating and cytoplasm-donating species. More recently, other researchers have been able to show that when species characteristics do appear in hybrid merogones of sea urchins, they are to a large extent paternal, after all.

The story of hybrid amphibian merogones has been one of similar achievements and disappointments. In Fig. 7a we show that, with the aid of a micropipette, one can remove the maternal nucleus (h) from the oocyte of the small palmate newt (*Triturus helveticus*). This egg had been previously inseminated with sperm (cr) from another species, the large crested newt (*Triturus cristatus*), so we now have a hybrid merogonic embryo in which the only maternal contribution is enucleated h-cytoplasm. The nuclear material comes entirely from the paternal side (cr). At best, such embryos develop as far as the stage (Fig. 7b) in which the first signs of the neural tube and optic vesicles become visible, and then die. These incompatible combinations of nucleus and cytoplasm from different species thus perish before any recognizable species-specific characteristics have appeared. There is nevertheless a trick which permits us to pursue the matter somewhat further. Before the merogone enters its final crisis, we remove a piece of superficial embryonic tissue (Fig. 7c) and implant it in a genetically healthy host embryo (d) from which—in order to make room for the implant—a corresponding piece of ectoderm has previously been

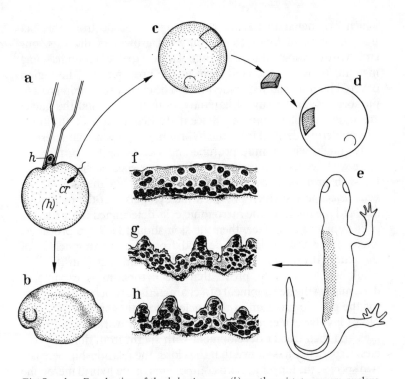

Fig. 7a—h. a Enucleation of the *helveticus* egg (*h*); *cr* the *cristatus* sperm nucleus. b Maximal development achievable by a (*h*)×*cr* merogone. c Donor of a piece of merogonic ectoderm. d Normal diploid host embryo (*Triturus alpestris*) with haploid implant (dotted). e Young metamorphosed newt with hybrid merogone flank epidermis. f Epidermis of *Triturus cristatus* with smooth surface. g Epidermis of the transplant shows characteristic protuberances and thus resembles the epidermis of a normal *Triturus helveticus* (h). (After E. Hadorn)

removed. The transplanted cells are marked with a vital dye (show dotted), which does not impair further development. The hope is that the small piece can perhaps survive that phase which is fatal for the merogone as a whole (b) if it is removed in time from its unhealthy environment to a normally developing system. Perhaps it will even be able to reach the stage at which distinctive species characteristics appear.

A fine example of a successful experiment of this kind is shown in Fig. 7e. The left flank of the host is covered with epidermis

21

which originated in the hybrid merogone. Aside from the fact that the implant hindered the outward growth of the legs, our embryo developed into a normal larva capable of undergoing metamorphosis to the land form at the proper time. The region covered by transplanted epidermis can be clearly seen in microscopic sections; as a result of haploidy, both the cells and the nuclei are much smaller than in adjacent diploid tissues of the host. The epidermis derived from the hybrid merogones is characteristically rough, with minute protuberances covering the surface (g). Here we have the expression of a distinctive species characteristic, for such protuberances are also to be found on the skin of the *helveticus* species which provided the cytoplasm of the merogone (h). Had the nuclei of the merogonic cells determined the structure of the epidermal surface, then the skin should lack the protuberances, since the nuclei are derived from the sperm nucleus of the paternal *cristatus* species, which has a smooth skin (f). This result would seem to prove that the cytoplasm is capable of determining the development of a characteristic which is not typical for the genetic program of the nucleus-donating species.

Nowadays we can enucleate the eggs of a great variety of amphibians and then trigger development with sperm from different species. Experience has shown that the closer the relationship between two species, the longer the two components of the hybrid merogone are able to work together. Thus, the combination of *Triturus helveticus* cytoplasm with a *Triturus taeniatus* nucleus dies only at a very advanced larval stage, i. e. at a much later stage than the merogone shown in Fig. 7b, where the *helveticus* cytoplasm was provided with a "more foreign" *cristatus* nucleus. On the other hand, newt cytoplasm containing the nucleus of a toad or a salamander can manage only the very first steps in development. Results such as these once again underscore the fact that the nucleus does not exercise sovereign control over development. Rather, the nuclear genes function in cooperation with the cytoplasm, which has species-specific qualities of its own. And so, when a hybrid merogone—sooner or later, depending on the combination—does founder in its attempts to meet the ever-increasing demands of continued development, the failure is due to an inability of nucleus and cytoplasm to "understand" each other any longer.

This is not to say, however, that such findings argue against the importance of the cell nucleus as carrier of the hereditary factors, the Mendelian genes. They merely set limits to the sphere of influence of the nucleus in determining specific developmental processes. As already mentioned (p. 20), there have also been many merogone experiments in which the nuclear genes have determined specific hereditary characteristics. These experiments have extended the known boundaries of the nuclear sphere of influence. In one such case, when the enucleated cytoplasm of the black axolotl is combined with a sperm nucleus derived from the white strain of axolotls, the merogone develops with paternally determined white color. Even in those merogone experiments in which cytoplasmically determined hereditary characteristics appear, it must be borne in mind that the egg cell was, after all, under the influence of a maternal nucleus during its growth and maturation phase. It is entirely possible—and, as we will show in the next chapter, it has been proved in individual cases (p. 35)—that, before the sperm nucleus even enters the picture, the cytoplasm of the oocyte has already been predetermined by maternal nuclear genes. Maternal characteristics in the new generation can therefore not be used to disprove a "nuclear monopoly" of the controlling factors operating in the developing animal. Unfortunately, we must conclude that merogone experiments do not permit a distinction between nucleus-dependent predetermination and autonomous cytoplasmic inheritance.

Functions of the Genetic Material during Oocyte Maturation

During embryonic development, as will be described in detail later (p. 98), the germ cells migrate into the gonadal *primordium* or *anlage*, the localized cell grouping destined to form the gonad. Once there, they enter upon one of two paths of differentiation, leading towards either egg or sperm. At the completion of metamorphosis (4—6 months in many amphibian species) the young newts and frogs are still very small. They grow quite slowly, and it takes two to three years for them to reach full size. Under the influence of the gonadotropic hormones of the hypophysis (p.

4), the gonads increase in size during this youthful phase and the germ cells develop into mature, fertile, gametes.

At the beginning of this process the germ cell nuclei of the newt, like the somatic cell nuclei, have twenty-four chromosomes, of which twelve are derived from the mother and twelve from the father. The chromosome complement is thus *diploid*—composed of two paired sets (Fig. 5g). During the process of germ cell maturation (gametogenesis) the chromosome number is reduced by half (cf. Fig. 34). The whole process, called *reduction division* or *meiosis*, is accomplished by the two maturation divisions mentioned earlier (Fig. 4). In the prophase of the first division, a crucial event takes place: corresponding (homologous) maternal and paternal chromosomes pair off with one another (as in Fig. 8 b). In the newt there are twelve such pairs. Each chromosome within a pair is in turn subdivided into two sister chromosomes, making a group of four chromosome strands in all, called a tetrad. The chromosomes of the tetrad are then distributed into future egg and sperm cells by means of two maturation divisions; this is accomplished in such a way that each mature gamete receives only a single *(haploid)* chromosome set of nonhomologous chromosomes. The mechanism of the meiotic divisions, which will not be described in detail here, assures that each individual chromosome, and hence each gene, is represented only once in the new set achieved by random assortment of paternal and maternal chromosomes.

In this chapter we want to examine the chromosomes of the amphibian oocyte during the prophase of meiosis and demonstrate that the functioning of the genetic material at this early stage is indispensable for the normal course of embryonic development. Once homologous chromosomes have paired successfully, they become extraordinarily elongated: in newts the length can reach one millimeter. At the same time lateral loops appear along the entire length of each chromosome (Fig. 8 b).

These shaggy looking chromosomes are called *lampbrush chromosomes*. They occur not only in the maturing amphibian oocyte, but also in fish and in other vertebrates. A lampbrush stage has recently been demonstrated for the human oocyte, as well.

More detailed investigations, primarily of newt oocytes, have revealed that individual loops are not randomly distributed. Large

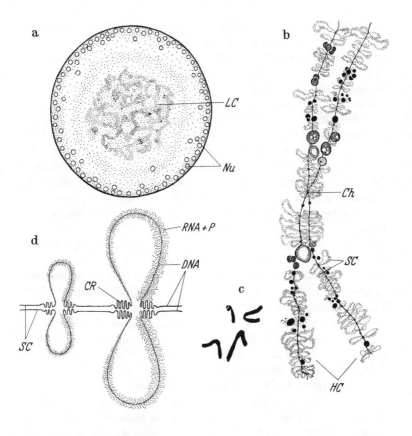

Fig. 8 a—d. Structure and function of lampbrush chromosomes: a—c for the crested newt *(Triturus cristatus)*. a Nucleus of a maturing oocyte: in the center of the nucleus, the tangled lampbrush chromosomes *(LC)*; on the nuclear periphery, numerous nucleoli *(Nu)*. b Detail of two paired homologous chromosomes *(HC)*; note the correspondence of the pattern of loops on the paired maternal and paternal chromosomes, which are held together at an attachment site or chiasma *(Ch)*. c Sizes and shapes of several typical chromosomes from normal somatic cells, drawn to the same scale as the parts of lampbrush chromosomes shown in b. d Diagram of the probable structure of a lampbrush chromosome, showing a single DNA molecule running the length of each of the paired sister chromatids *(SC)*, the condensed regions *(CR)* and the increasing accumulation of *RNA* and protein along the loops *(RNA + P)*. (a—c after H.C. Callan, d modified from various authors)

25

loops and small, thicker ones and thinner ones, as well as knot-like regions, can be distinguished. Within a given species, they always appear at the same place on the chromosome (Fig. 8b), forming distinctive patterns which permit identification of each of the twelve chromosomes. There are several hundred loops per chromosome; taking all the chromosomes together, there are some 5,000 points at which loops protrude. Looking at two paired homologous chromosomes (*HS*) in Fig. 8b, we note the same symmetrical pattern of loops in the sister chromatids (*SC*, Figs. 8b and d) derived from each of them. The lampbrush stage lasts many months. Then the loops regress completely and the chromosomes shorten, reassuming their usual appearance (Fig. 8c).

We can now ask whether this striking change in chromosome structure during the lampbrush stage is related to a special function of the chromosomal material during this phase of oocyte maturation. The answer is yes, but to understand what this function is we must first acquaint ourselves with some of the fundamental results of the "new genetics" which is concerned with the molecular basis of gene action. Our aim here is to present a brief sketch only—the reader should consult a modern text in genetics or molecular biology for details and for an account of the exciting course of research which has, in a remarkably short time, established the "facts" we shall summarize here.

In higher organisms, such as the Amphibia, some tens of thousands of genes act as carriers of information and as functional units. The actual material of which the genes are made is a long helical molecule composed of two intertwined strands, called deoxyribonucleic acid or DNA. Each strand of this molecule is a long chain-like sequence of "bases", made from four different building blocks called nucleotides. Base-pair interactions help to hold the strands together: any given base can pair with only one of the other three base types; no base can pair with another like itself. The two DNA strands are able to bind together along their entire lengths because they have *complementary* sequences—the place on the other strand opposite any given base will always be occupied by that one base with which it is capable of forming a base pair. The second strand is thus a linear sequence of base-pairing partners complementary to the first strand. Each gene is several hundred to a thousand nucleotides in length. And since within

26

the length of an average gene an essentially unlimited number of compositions and arrangements of the four nucleotide building blocks is possible, each one of the many different genes can have its own unique base sequence.

The information stored in the DNA is *transcribed* onto a strand of a related molecule called ribonucleic acid (RNA). Each of the four RNA building blocks is capable of base-pair interaction with one (but only one) of the bases in DNA. With a single DNA strand serving as template, a complementary sequence of RNA nucleotides is laid down. Because of the specificity of complementary base-pair interactions, all the information contained in the linear sequence of bases in a single DNA strand is faithfully transcribed onto the complementary RNA sequence. Several kinds of RNA can be distinguished according to their subsequent functions. One category of genes encodes a kind of RNA called "messenger RNA" (mRNA). This mRNA generally leaves the cell nucleus and serves "on the outside", in the cytoplasm, as template for the synthesis of protein chains. Some twenty different amino acids are available as building blocks for making proteins. They are joined to one another in a specific sequence determined by the sequence of bases in the mRNA. Triplets of three adjacent bases form the codewords for the different amino acids (for further details of this process, see below). In this process the base sequence language of the nucleic acids is *translated* into the amino acid sequence language of the proteins. The practically unlimited multiplicity of different mRNA template sequences makes possible in turn a nearly unlimited variety of different protein molecules. What significance do the proteins, the products of the translation machinery, have for the life of the cell? Some amino acid chains serve as structural elements within the cell; they are components of different fibers and membranes. Other proteins function as hormones, while globin chains combine to form oxygen-carrying blood pigments (p. 123). But most of the proteins coded for by the mRNA function as enzymes. Underlying the life process and insuring its integrity are thousands of metabolic steps, and every one of these chemical reactions in the cell is made possible by the action of a specific enzyme.

The translation process which produces the proteins is carried out at specific subcellular structures or organelles which look like little balls in electron micrographs. Because they were found to be rich in RNA, the structures were called "ribosomes". Their "ribosomal RNA" (rRNA) differs from mRNA in several characteristic respects including molecular size. The special ribosomal genes which code for rRNA are, as we shall see, located at very particular places on certain chromosomes: it is at these DNA regions that the nucleolus is organized anew at each cell division (Figs. 9c, 9d). Transcribed rRNA first collects in the nucleoli and is then distributed throughout the cell.

Transfer RNA (tRNA) is the last type of RNA we need to mention. Like mRNA and rRNA, tRNA molecules are base sequences complementary to a particular class of genes. Each of the various tRNA molecules becomes coupled in a selective, enzyme-catalyzed, process to one of the twenty kinds of amino acid, resulting in a "charged tRNA". Besides possessing an amino acid binding site, each tRNA molecule has a special sequence of three bases complementary to that mRNA triplet which codes for the selectively bound amino acid. At the ribosome these amino acid-charged linker molecules arrange themselves by complementary base pairing according to the sequence of mRNA triplets, thus feeding the amino acid chain polymerizing machinery with the correct sequence of amino acids. These molecular processes are summarized in Table 1.

Now we can return to the lampbrush chromosomes and see how they fit into this scheme of molecular events common to every living cell. It has been established that the strands of a single giant DNA molecule run the length of the chromosome. This

Table 1. Functions of the genetic material: Different classes of genes in the DNA code for different kinds of RNA.
(Abbreviations are explained in the text)

Genes $\xrightarrow{\text{Transcription}}$	RNA $\xrightarrow{\text{Translation}}$	Proteins
Some DNA codes for	mRNA	which is translated into structural proteins and enzymes
Some DNA codes for	rRNA	which serves as part of the protein-synthesizing machinery
Some DNA codes for	tRNA	which brings amino acids to the site of protein synthesis

DNA double helix runs out on to each loop, where it is visible as the central thread, and then back in again, as depicted in Fig. 8d. It has also been demonstrated that the loops are particularly active sites of RNA (and also protein) accumulation, indicating that the looped regions of the DNA contain actively transcribing genes. Although several thousand loops exist, it is possible to calculate that the genes active in the loops comprise no more than 3—5% of all genes. The remainder of the genes evidently comes into play only later, as the embryo is developing into a larva and eventually into an adult.

The gene activity of lampbrush chromosomes has been further characterized. First, it is now known that the active genes provide the oocyte with particularly long-lived mRNA molecules which become translated into proteins only well after fertilization has taken place. For amphibians, and for sea urchins as well, it has been shown that the first developmental stages—cleavage and blastulation to the beginning of gastrulation (Figs. 11, 16)—proceed in the absence of new gene activity, i.e. in the absence of new DNA-dependent RNA synthesis. Throughout these early stages the embryo uses the transcribed material stored up for it during the maturation of the oocyte. Second, during the lampbrush chromosome stage, extra DNA is synthesized which accumulates within the nucleus. The particles which result from this process contain "amplified" copies of many hundreds of ribosomal genes (p. 32). These then serve as templates for the transcription of the rRNA destined to become part of the ribosome structure. Such DNA-containing particles become incorporated into the numerous nucleoli which appear during the lampbrush stage, particularly at the periphery of the nucleus (Fig. 8a). There are several hundred of these oocyte nucleoli in the newt. In the clawed frog, the oocyte nucleoli come to number more than a thousand while the other cell types usually have only two nucleoli per cell. Thus provided with a rich ribosomal dowry, the egg cell is ready, once the lampbrush chromosomes have regressed, to enter the phase of fertilization and early development.

With this general picture of the genetic activity of lampbrush chromosomes in mind, we now want to introduce two specific examples to show that gene activity occurring during the lampbrush stage is vital for the first steps in the life of the next generation.

A mutant of the clawed frog *Xenopus* was discovered by chance at the University of Oxford. Chromosomes bearing this mutation, which is inherited like any other Mendelian gene, form no nucleolus. The mutant gene is designated *onu* (for "no nucleolus"),

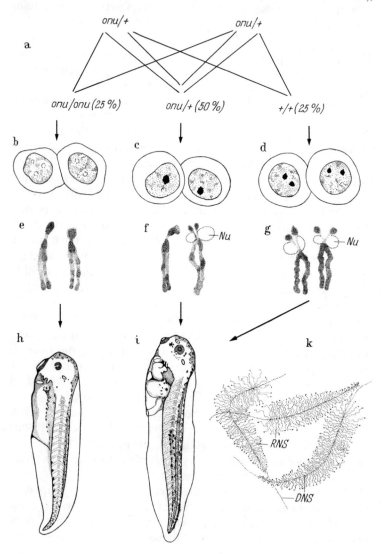

while the symbol + is used to designate the non-mutated normal gene. Starting with parents each possessing one *onu* and one + gene (heterozygous condition) we can arrive at the probability (p) for each possible genotype in their progeny (Fig. 9a): p = 1/4 for homozygous *onu/onu* individuals; p = 1/2 for heterozygotes (*onu*/+); and p = 1/4 for homozygous normals (+/+). Individuals of the *onu/onu* class form no nucleoli (Fig. 9b), the *onu*/+ individuals form a single nucleolus (Fig. 9c), and the homozygous normal individuals form two nucleoli per cell. Figs. 9e through 9g show that elaboration of the nucleolus proceeds from a distinctly constricted region called the "nucleolus organizer", located on one of the eighteen chromosomal pairs to be found in *Xenopus* nuclei. In the *onu* mutant this region is considerably shortened and its nucleolus organizer capability is lost (Figs. 9e, 9f).

The *onu/onu* individuals survive at first. But they proceed through early development only as far as the clearly abnormal stage shown in Fig. 9h, with the eyes consistently undersized, the gut hardly developed and the tail bent over at the end. At this stage, without exception, they die. Their ability to survive the initial developmental stages is evidently only made possible by the fact that oocyte maturation occurred in a heterozygous mother where one nucleolus organizer was still available. In the *onu*/+ female a supply of rRNA can be accumulated during the lampbrush stage and later supplied to *onu* and + oocytes alike. This supply lasts into larval development, and only when it runs out does the lethal effect of the *onu* mutant become evident. Siblings of the mutant larvae, as long as they possess at least one nucleolus organizer, develop normally.

Those molecular biologists concerned with the synthesis and function of rRNA have been understandably eager to exploit the

---

◀ Fig. 9 a—k. Function of a specific chromosome region as nucleolus organizer in the clawed frog *Xenopus laevis*. A Mendelian segregation in the progeny of a mating between two parents heterozygous for the *onu* (no nucleolus) factor; cells of offspring contain no nucleoli (b), one nucleolus (c) or two nucleoli (d). e—g Microscopic appearance of the chromosome pair responsible for nucleolus (*Nu*) formation. h Anucleolate larva just before its death. i Normal control larva of the same age. k Three ribosomal genes as found in nucleoli at the lampbrush stage. RNA is transcribed along the central DNA strand. (b—i after M. Fischberg and co-workers, in part unpublished; k after O. L. Miller and B. R. Beatty)

possibilities opened up to them by the availability of mutants at a known chromosomal locus responsible for nucleolus formation. It was soon established that rRNA synthesis involves more than just a single gene. In *Xenopus* and in newts, as well as in the fruit fly *Drosophila*, it has been established that hundreds

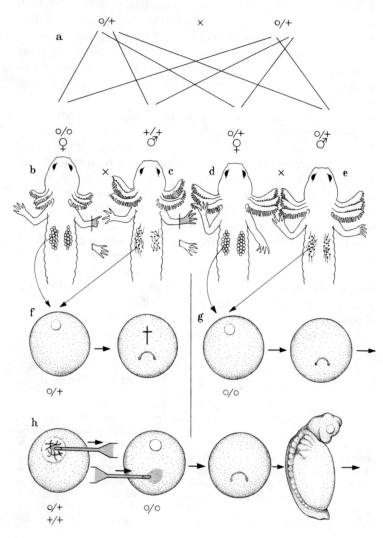

of genes in the DNA all perform the same function, transcribing their identical information onto rRNA molecules, which are then available to the cell in great quantities. Evidently the need for these molecules in the constant renewal of the millions of ribosomes is so great that the necessary level of production cannot be achieved by a single copy of the gene for rRNA. Recently, using the electron microscope, American researchers have succeeded in observing and photographing the rRNA-transcribing genes in maturing oocytes (Fig. 9k). Along DNA strands of equal length we can see characteristic patterns of fine threadlike projections. These are "growing" RNA molecules, precursors of rRNA. Each DNA segment is a single ribosomal RNA gene of the oocyte. Since the length of the RNA threads increases along the gene, we can assume that RNA transcription is initiated at a specific site and then proceeds along the gene. As soon as the initiation site is unoccupied a new strand is started.

The genes shown in Fig. 9k occur in great numbers in all the many nucleoli which form during the lampbrush stage (Fig. 8a). In later stages the ribosomal genes no longer detach from the nucleolus organizer but remain attached at the constriction shown in Figs. 9f and 9g and function at that spot. In *Xenopus* there are approximately 600 identical functional units arrayed in tandem along the DNA strand, all of them coding for ribosomal RNA. The second gene which has been important in elucidating the function of the lampbrush stage was discovered in the axolotl (*Ambystoma mexicanum*). In a strain of these laboratory animals larvae were observed which show somewhat slower growth than normal animals. In addition they have shorter gills and are incapable of complete regeneration after limb amputation (Fig. 10b),

---

◀ Fig. 10a—h. The o gene (ovaries defective) in the axolotl (*Ambystoma mexicanum*). a Cross between two parents heterozygous for o and segregation in the offspring. b × c A homozygous o/o female mated with a +/+ male produces o/+ eggs (f) which survive only as far as early gastrula (†=death). d × e Cross between heterozygotes produces 25% homozygous o/o offspring (g) which develop normally. h Removal of "normal" nuclear sap at the lampbrush stage of eggs from o/+ or +/+ mothers and injection into eggs from o/o mothers leads to normal development (arrows). Comparison of b and c shows the difference in regeneration capacity; regenerated extremity shown dotted. (After R.R. Humphrey and after R. Briggs and J.T. Justus)

whereas the normal axolotl possesses a very high regeneration capacity (Fig. 10c).

Using cross mating experiments it was possible (Fig. 10a) to show that the poorly regenerating animals were homozygous for a mutant gene. This mutation is designated o because, as we shall see, the ovaries of homozygotes are affected as well.

In a mating between two heterozygous +/o parents (Figs. 10a, 10d, 10e) one fourth of the offspring will be o/o individuals which can develop into viable larvae impaired solely in their capability for regeneration and in their germ cell development. In o/o males this germ cell impairment causes sterility due to lack of functional sperm, while o/o females are fertile. If the latter are crossed with +/+ males, the resulting o/+ embryos develop only as far as early gastrula (Fig. 10f) and then die. Because viable o/+ heterozygotes exist, however, we know that the genotype of the zygotes cannot be responsible for their early death. The decisive factor must be the o/o genotype of the mother.

Thus far we can sum up as follows: a fertilized o egg is only capable of development if it is derived from an o/+ mother; should it happen to have matured inside an o/o mother it is condemned to an early death. An experiment was designed to test whether it was the ovary alone which was crucial to the developmental potential of the egg or whether some sort of metabolic defect in the rest of the maternal organism could be the determining factor. First, young +/+ ovaries were implanted into o/o hosts. They produced completely normal eggs. But then in the reverse experiment, with o/o ovaries implanted into +/+ hosts, the effect of the normal host environment was inadequate to prevent early death of embryos derived from the o/o ovary. The life-or-death decision evidently is made directly and autonomously in the ovary or in the oocyte itself. But in what respect do the oocytes in o/o mothers differ from those in o/+ and +/+ mothers?

At the lampbrush stage the nucleus (germinal vesicle) of an o/+ or +/+ oocyte can be pricked with a micropipette and the nuclear sap drawn off (Fig. 10h). This sample can then be injected into an otherwise doomed o/o egg. The result is striking: the injected nuclear sap has a lifesaving effect and the animal now survives the critical lethal phase. Many embryos develop much further:

they make it through gastrulation, become neurulae, and some are even able to proceed through the whole of larval development. In a few cases, then, their accomplishments approach those of an o/o embryo derived from an o/+ mother.

The lifegiving factor can also be obtained at later stages in oogenesis, after the lampbrush loops have regressed and the nuclear membrane has broken down, i. e. after the nuclear sap has been mixed with the cytoplasm. Smaller amounts of it can even be prepared from cleavage and blastula stages of the early embryo. Extracts of later stages are without effect, however,

By testing various cell fractions, it can be concluded that the lifesaving substance does not occur in any preformed cell structures and organelles, such as ribosomes or mitochondria. The molecule in question can be neither DNA or RNA, since treatment with nucleic acid digesting enzymes fails to destroy the biological activity. Heating and treatment with proteolytic enzymes destroy the activity, indicating that the active substance is a protein. This indicates that in the lampbrush stage the normal (+) gene is active, transcribing its information onto a specific RNA, which in turn codes for a specific protein chain. If only o genes are present the synthesis of this substance cannot occur.

This gene-determined substance is formed inside the maternal organism prior to fertilization but becomes operational only at the time of gastrulation. A normal gene introduced by a + sperm cannot make up for deficient production of this substance. In the case just described we have a fine example of *maternal effect* or *predetermination* (see p. 23) in which properties of the coming generation are determined as a result of gene activity in the oocyte before fertilization. Purely maternal genetic effects on development are known for many different genes in almost every kind of organism. They teach us that the destiny of the new generation is initially determined not at fertilization, but earlier. Genes showing such maternal effects apparently comprise only a small fraction of all the genes, however. For the majority of genes the contributions of sperm and egg are of equal importance.

The o-mutant calls our attention to another problem of general importance. It looks as if a given gene need not be in operation constantly, but can be temporally restricted, i. e. phase-specific, in its activity. The + gene of the axolotl is clearly functional during the lampbrush stage, then seems to be dormant early in post-fertilization development. It certainly becomes active again somewhat later on. This second round of activity is clearly indicated by the subnormal performance of the older o/o larvae (Fig. 10b) in contrast to o/+ or +/+ larvae (Fig. 10c and d). The genes active in the maturing oocyte are mainly those—like the normal gene at the o locus—which code for substances required in the early stages of development preceding gastrulation, when, as we shall see (p. 43), no gene transcription takes place and the developing organism lives from stored materials. As transcription resumes along with gastrulation, new kinds of mRNA are formed and new populations of proteins—mainly enzymes—are coded for and synthesized. At this point both paternal and maternal genes are in operation.

One of the central tasks facing modern developmental biology is to unravel all the mechanisms which control the timing of gene action and to find out how, in the different cell systems of an organism, different teams of genes become turned on or off.

From One Cell to Many

Every multicellular organism begins its life as a single cell—everything begins with the fertilized egg. All the maternal and paternal genes are united in the zygote nucleus; all the specific construction elements and storage materials have been assembled in the cytoplasm. In the fertilized egg, therefore, everything is on hand which is essential for determination and guidance of the individual's initial development. By the time development has been completed the organism is composed of an unimaginably large number of cells: in the human the estimated total is a number with fifteen zeros. How then does a multicellular animal emerge from just a single cell? What kind of distribution of the information in the genetic material takes place? How is it that one cell becomes a nerve cell and another a gland cell?

Let's see first what we can learn from outward appearances (Fig. 11). In the newt, a furrow appears at the animal pole of the egg some five hours after fertilization. This deepening furrow

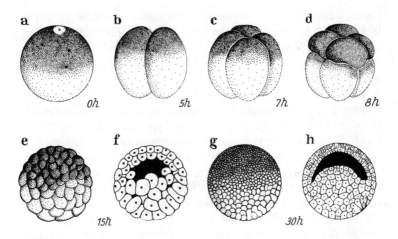

Fig. 11a—h. Cleavage of the egg of the alpine newt (*Triturus alpestris*). The times in hours (h) are for a temperature of 18 °C. a The unfertilized egg (cf. Fig. 4). b—d Two-, four-, and eight-cell stages. e External view of a morula. f Section through a morula showing the blastocoel (black) as it begins to form. g External view of a blastula. h Section through a blastula

extends rapidly around both sides of the egg, soon reaching the equator and then the vegetal pole (b). One or two hours after this first cleavage through the egg has been completed a second furrow appears perpendicular to the first cleavage plane (c). The second cleavage produces a stage with four equally large cleavage cells or *blastomeres*. The third cleavage is not longitudinal, from pole to pole, but follows a parallel of latitude somewhat to the animal side of the equator; it thus produces an eight cell stage comprised of four smaller "animal" cells and four larger "vegetal" cells (d). Further cleavages, more or less synchronous, divide the egg into smaller and smaller pieces, and by about fifteen hours after fertilization the embryo comes to look (Fig. 11c) like a mulberry (*Morus*), hence the name *morula* given to this stage. On the second day after fertilization, after 13—14 rounds of cell division the embryo contains some 8,000—16,000 cells, by now microscopically small. At this point the cleavage divisions come to an end, resulting in an embryonic stage called a *blastula* (g).

During cleavage, cells separate from one another so that the inside of the blastula comes to have a well defined hollow space, the *blastocoel* (Figs. 11f, 11h). The smaller animal cells form the roof of the cavity while the thick floor is formed by the large yolk-laden vegetal cells.

A nuclear division precedes each cell cleavage. All organisms employ a similar mechanism to ensure an equivalent distribution of the genetic material. For the newt this means that the twelve maternal and twelve paternal chromosomes brought together at fertilization must be exactly duplicated before each division, making available twenty-four daughter pairs. The mitotic apparatus distributes one member of each pair to each daughter nucleus, so that each daughter nucleus contains a diploid set of twenty-four chromosomes, twelve each of maternal and paternal origin. This process is repeated at every subsequent nuclear division preceding a cell division. The multicellular organism which results has millions of cells and every one of them is equipped with the entire genetic heritage provided by the parent sperm and egg.

But are these daughter nuclei really all identical? Could every one of them, if forced to, take over the role of the nucleus in the fertilized, but still uncleaved, egg? Do they still have all the necessary information to guide the development of a whole individual?

Hans Spemann designed an experiment to get at this important question. While fertilized newt eggs were still at the one cell stage he constricted them into a barbell shape (Fig. 12). The diploid nucleus is thus "tied off" in one of the two halves, and it is this half alone (provided the other half contains no supernumerary nuclei resulting from polyspermy) which begins cleavage (a, right). When development in this half has reached the eight cell or sixteen cell stage (b), one of the cleavage nuclei can pass over into the uncleaved egg half, after which the loop is pulled tight, completely separating the two halves. In the part which has already been cleaving, development continues normally, leading in favorable cases to a complete, normally viable, larva (c, right). The egg half which was only later provided with an "older" cleavage nucleus also begins to divide, and from this half, too, a completely normal larva can emerge (c, left). The slight retardation in development still visible in Fig. 12 is of no importance later on.

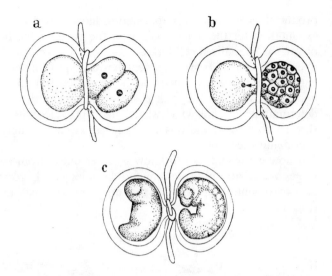

Fig. 12a—c. Delayed provision of nucleus to one side of a constricted newt egg. a Two-cell stage. b At an advanced cleavage stage a nucleus is able to pass over into the uncleaved half (arrow). c Twin larvae: both are normal, but the one on the left (having started cleavage only after an initial delay) has still not quite caught up in its development. (After H. Spemann)

To appreciate the importance of Spemann's accomplishment, we must realize that it sounded the death knell of an enormously influential theory of development promulgated by August Weismann in 1892. This great biological theoretician had taught that only in the zygote nucleus were all the genetic factors, all the developmental determinants, still intact and united. Thereafter an orderly but unequal distribution of these factors would be achieved through egg cleavage—each daughter nucleus would get only a selected fraction of that which the parent nucleus had contained. Accordingly, the first nuclear division would distribute to one daughter nucleus those determinants necessary for the development of the right half of the organism while the other would receive all those necessary for the left half. Every subsequent division would bring about further restrictions in the complement of determinants. Finally, cells having nuclei containing only the genes for, say, musculature or particular sense organs would be produced. Weismann thus appeared to have provided an elegant explanation for the differentiation of the parts of the body and of various specialized cell types.

Spemann's constriction experiment, however, proved that the cleavage nuclei are equivalent at least up to the sixteen cell stage and, moreover, that they still possess a full set of developmental determinants. The half which was belatedly provided with a nucleus showed no defects, and this completeness argues strongly against Weismann's teachings.

But now we would like to know whether nuclei from even later stages are capable of promoting full development. In recent times an experimental approach to this question has been developed (Fig. 13).

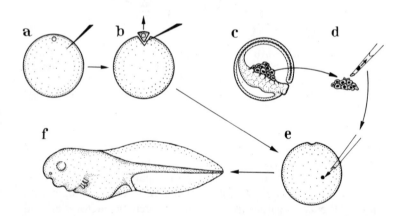

Fig. 13a—f. Enucleated frog eggs are provided with nuclei from advanced developmental stages. a Activation of the egg. b Removal of the egg nucleus. c A gastrula serves as nucleus donor. d Drawing a cell nucleus into the pipette. e Injection of the nucleus. f Young tadpole derived from the injected egg (e). (Adapted from R. Briggs and T. J. King)

An unfertilized frog egg is first pricked with a needle (a), a stimulus necessary in order to activate the egg for further development. Then the nucleus of the egg cell is teased out and away from the egg (b). Next the experimenter removes a group of cells from a developmentally advanced stage, e. g. from a late gastrula (c). In our Fig. 13 the cells taken are endodermal cells from the archenteron floor (see Fig. 16). A single one of these is drawn up into a micropipette (d); this causes the body of the cell to rupture and become partially stripped away from the nucleus. The nucleus to be tested can now be injected into the enucleated egg (e). The "young" egg cytoplasm furnished with an "old" cell nucleus soon begins cleavage. Subsequent development can lead to a completely normal and highly developed tadpole (f).

Cell nuclei with the "experience" of early development now far behind them are thus capable of "taking it from the top" once more. This can only mean that the nucleus from an older embryo is still *totipotent*, retaining the full range of developmental potencies present in the zygote nucleus. Differential distribution of hereditary factors has therefore not taken place and the cell nucleus has evidently not (or, at least, not yet) become irreversibly specialized for a single function. Along with these successful cases, however, there are many embryos which don't make it very far at all after the older nucleus has been injected. We must now pay proper attention to these failures, as well.

To do this we shall consider another experimental series, this time with the clawed frog *(Xenopus laevis)*. The advanced embryonic stage which serves as nuclear donor is shown in Fig. 14 *(D I)*; this stage is called a neurula, an embryo in which the folds of the brain and spinal cord have become prominent (see Fig. 17, p. 51). Nuclei were obtained from cells taken from an area which later would have formed the body musculature. Great differences were observed in the development of uncleaved egg cells provided with these "old" nuclei *(G I)*. Two embryos stopped development at the blastula stage. Eight other embryos gave rise to hopelessly deformed embryos and larvae. More or less normal larvae developed in three cases and in two eggs harmonious development right through metamorphosis was brought about by a neurula nucleus.

A parallel experiment indicated that the injected nuclei taken from the donor *(D I)* possessed widely different developmental potencies. At the blastula stage, i. e. before any developmental crisis would have been reached, two embryos from among the *G I* "siblings" were selected to serve as second round nuclear

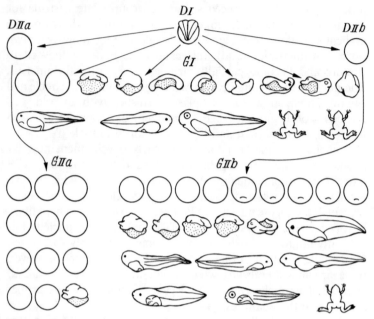

Fig. 14. Serial nuclear transplantation in eggs of the clawed frog (*Xenopus laevis*). *DI* donor of the first-generation nuclei. *G I* differential developmental performance with nuclei from *DI*. *DIIa* and *DIIb* blastulae with nuclei derived from *DI* which serve as second-round nuclei donors. *GIIa* and *GIIb* developmental performance with nuclei from *DIIa* and *DIIb*, respectively. (Adapted from M. Fischberg, J. B. Gurdon, and T. R. Elsdale)

donors (*D IIa, D IIb*). Of the twelve embryos which developed with nuclei derived from *D IIa*, all but one ceased development at the blastula stage (*G IIa*). The eggs provided with *D IIb* nuclei, on the other hand, showed a range in developmental performance similar to that of the first transplant generation *G I*. It seemed, therefore, that the nuclei of the neurula were no longer equivalent.

Further investigations done recently, however, have shown that in a high proportion of cases there is damage to the nuclei due to the hazards of the transplantation technique. This becomes manifest later on as the nuclei divide, by the appearance of chromosome breaks and abnormal chromosome distribution at cell division. Normal developmental performance simply cannot be expected of nuclei when they have such gross defects in their genetic material. What this means is that the differences between the two populations *G IIa* and *G IIb* may reflect nothing more than differential damage to the two nuclei implanted into *D IIa* and *D IIb*: no conclusions may be drawn concerning differences in the nuclei of the donor (*D I*) cells. There is still the possibility that, along with the failures attributable to externally caused damage, the failure of some transplants to develop might reflect real restrictions in potency—nuclei in certain parts of the differentiating embryo having been modified in such a way that they can no longer "find their way back". And while we now realize that *negative* results from transplantation experiments cannot be used to argue for this possibility, there are recent *positive* results which argue against it. It has been possible to isolate nuclei from unmistakably differentiated intestinal cells of *Xenopus* tadpoles, and after transplantation into enucleated eggs, to achieve development of metamorphosed, sexually mature, clawed frogs. Even nuclei transplanted from cultures of adult-derived skin cells function smoothly in the ooplasm, giving rise to normal tadpoles with all their many cell types. Yet the progenitors of these diverse cells were all of one type: specialized keratin-producing skin cells. The "old" nucleus readjusts its functions to the early embryonic conditions of its new cytoplasmic environment. Its genetic material reenacts the drama of development on a new stage. Astonishingly, even nuclei from the brains of adult frogs, when introduced into the cytoplasm of enucleated eggs, are able to react to the completely new environment. They swell and begin to synthesize DNA as is characteristic for the early embryonic phase. The ooplasm can thus reinitiate processes which were no longer active in the cells from which the nuclei were taken.

In another experiment, the opposite reaction was demonstrated— genes which had been active in a larval donor were turned off by the young egg cytoplasm. Implanted nuclei transcribe no rRNA during the period of cleavage whereas they had previously been intensively occupied with the production of this material. Such program changes are probably brought about by the influence of specific proteins in the egg cytoplasm.

While ever deepening insights into the mysteries of differentiation will come with the results of future experiments, we can now place the roles of nucleus and cytoplasm into a certain framework. It does not seem possible that unequal distribution of the genetic information can be responsible for the fact that the cells of an organism differ so greatly in form and function. According to everything we know now, the decisive switches that direct genetically identical cells onto tracks headed for different destinations must be thrown by *differences in the cytoplasm.* A cell nucleus which finds itself in a relatively yolk-free "animal" cytoplasm will experience different interactions than a brother nucleus surrounded by yolk-rich "vegetal" cytoplasm.

Regions of cytoplasm might differ, for example, in their content of enzymes necessary for the functioning of certain genes. And once established, a difference like this, however insignificant it may seem, can be the necessary first step on the way toward larger and more far-reaching differences. The assumption here is that the genes of the cell nucleus tend to enhance the differentness of the cytoplasm in which they come to lie, with such a process leading eventually to a muscle cell on the one hand and to a nerve cell on the other.

The essential significance of the cleavages now becomes clear. The large body of egg cytoplasm is divided into thousands of portions; the parcel of cytoplasm to which a nucleus is assigned may be larger or smaller, yolk-rich or yolk-poor, at the surface or buried. Within these small, defined, fields of action, development can follow a great variety of paths, depending on which few genes become active out of the full gene inventory available in every cell. Starting with the cytoplasmic differences established at cleavage it is possible to conceive of a sequence of nucleocytoplasmic interactions which would eventually construct an organism having numerous differentiated cell systems.

Formative Movements

If one cracks open a fertilized chicken egg after one day's incubation one will find a tiny flat embryonic disc spread upon the ball of yolk. Closer inspection reveals that the embryo is comprised of three sheets of cells. The topmost layer, the *ectoderm*, gives rise to the epidermis and the nervous system. The middle layer is the *mesoderm*—its cell produce skeleton, musculature, circulatory system, gonads and kidneys. Innermost we find the *endoderm*, from which develop the digestive tract, the liver, the lungs and other internal organs.

These three "germ layers" can be distinguished in all vertebrates. Their formation is in every case the result of a fundamental process which we will now follow in detail using the newt egg as an example. We saw how the cleavage divisions led to the formation of a hollow ball of cells called the blastula (Fig. 11). Subsequent to this the embryonic cells of the blastula begin to move in very specific directions. But because the embryo retains its basic spherical shape during this whole process it is quite difficult to follow these movements satisfactorily. The anatomist W. Vogt devised an elegant method to permit direct tracing of the paths followed by the moving cells. The surface of the embryo is tatooed at specific points using harmless "vital dyes" such as nile blue sulfate or neutral red. Small cubes of agar, a gelatin-like substance derived from marine algae, are first impregnated with dye and are then pressed against the surface of the embryo. The dye diffuses rapidly into the cells near the point of contact. Any desired spot on the embryo surface can be marked in this way (Fig. 16). The colored spots remain intact for weeks so that the movements of a dyed group of cells can be followed to their destination in a differentiated organ. One can determine where in the blastula the precursors of the lens of the eye, of the liver, or of a particular muscle segment had been located.

On the basis of numerous such markings a detailed "fate map" can be constructed (Fig. 15). It shows us where the materials for later organs were located prior to the formative, or morphogenetic, movements. The first important result of such investigations was to establish that the primordia for all the organs (and thus for the three germ layers) lie adjacent to one another on the embryo's surface.

Color marker studies also showed how the gut endoderm finds its way to the inside and how the primordia of the musculature, of the nervous system, and of all the other organ systems, assume their proper places in a multilayered embryo. The whole process, which occurs in some form or other in all multicellular animals, is called *gastrulation*: a simple hollow ball (blastula) is transformed into a layered hollow vessel (gastrula).

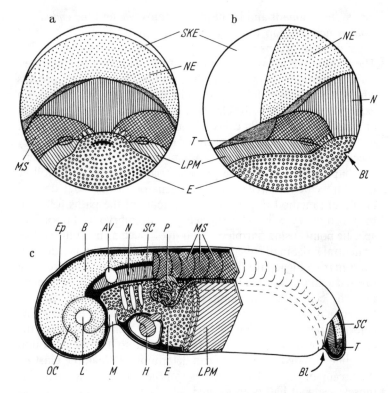

Fig. 15a—c. Amphibian fate map of an early gastrula (a and b) constructed by following marked cells into the various tissues and organs of the advanced embryo (c). a External view from the rear, showing the centrally located blastopore. b and c Views from the left side; *Bl* = site of blastopore. 1. *Ectodermal derivatives:* *SKE* skin ectoderm (white) forms epidermis (*Ep*), lens (*L*), auditory vesicle (*AV*), lining of mouth cavity (*M*); *NE* neural ectoderm (dotted) forms neural tube including brain (*B*), spinal cord (*SC*) and optic cup (*OC*). 2. *Mesodermal derivatives:* *N* notochord (vertical hatching), *MS* muscle segments (somites, diagonal hatching), *LPM* lateral plate mesoderm (cross hatching), *P* pronephros, *H* heart, *T* tail bud. 3. *Endoderm* (*E*, small circles) occupies the vegetal region of the early gastrula (a and b) and later forms the gut. Three gill slits (white) in the anterior part of the gut (c)

As first external indication of such morphogenetic movements a shallow depression appears below the equator on one side of the egg. This blastopore (*Bp*) (Fig. 15b) serves as our point of orientation. It defines the mid-plane of the animal and also allows us to tell front from rear and left from right. In vertebrates the opening at the blastopore eventually becomes the anal or cloacal orifice, for—as we shall see shortly—development of the archenteron (primitive gut cavity) proceeds from rear to front.

Let us now follow the gastrulation movements with the help of Fig. 16. Three dye spots (Fig. 16a, 1—3) are placed along the meridian which passes through the blastopore region (crescent "*Bp*" in early gastrula a), and two further spots (4 and 5) are placed at the equator on the circumference of a meridian perpendicular to the one which passes through the blastopore. Marker 1 lies at the animal pole, marker 3 at the vegetal pole, while marker 2 lies just above the blastopore. Looking at our tatooed embryo six hours later (Fig. 16b), we see that the shape of the blastopore has changed. Its borders surround the yolky material of the vegetal pole (marker 3). Marker 2 has almost completely disappeared beneath the surface and the other marked areas have also moved towards the edges of the blastopore. A section through this yolk plug stage (Fig. 16b, right) shows us the new positions taken up within the embryo by cells originally located on the surface. A new cavity has formed: the archenteron (*AC*). The roof of the archenteron (*AR*) is composed of cells which lay originally above the dorsal, or upper lip of the blastopore (marker 2). The floor of the archenteron, on the other hand, is formed from vegetal cells. The blastocoel (*Bc*) which was still quite spacious at the beginning of gastrulation is now literally forced up against the wall. After eight more hours, gastrulation is almost completely finished. The blastopore is now slit-shaped (Fig. 16c). The entire endoderm has now invaginated. Marker 2 is located in the roof of the future foregut. In addition, the two laterally marked areas 4 and 5 have moved to the edge of the blastopore and then, except for small leftover patches, have turned the corner and disappeared inside. The cells which stream over the surface toward the blastopore and then stream away from the blastopore again on the inside perform a sort of countermarch. Only the marked cells from the animal pole (1) remain entirely on the surface; their area has, however, been stretched out lengthwise in the direction of the blastopore.

At the end of gastrulation the three germ layers have reached
their definitive locations. The thick mass of endoderm with an

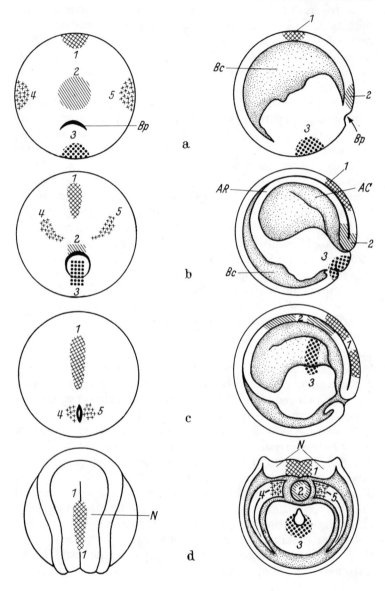

a

b

c

d

open dorsal groove covers the floor of the archenteron. The lateral wings of the endoderm will soon come together, forming the gut tube (Fig. 16d). The mesoderm lies spread out above the endoderm, with its overhanging ends forming the roof of the archenteron. Shortly after gastrulation this mesodermal cell mass will become divided into the primordia for notochord, muscle segments (somites) and kidneys. Only the ectoderm is left on the outside. Whereas before gastrulation the cells of this outermost germ layer covered just half of the embryo's surface (Figs. 15a, 15b), at the end of gastrulation they cover the whole embryo. Obviously, considerable stretching and flattening of the ectoderm must have occurred.

It cannot be our task in this small book to describe in an orderly way all the formative morphogenetic processes of subsequent development. Indeed, in discussing gastrulation we have explained only those features which will be necessary in order to understand certain key experiments.

As a further preparation, however, we must briefly explain a process of morphogenetic movements in the ectoderm, one that is set in motion only after gastrulation has ceased. This process leads to the separation of the neural ectoderm from the rest of the ectodermal mass, and to the formation of the nervous system. The remaining (non-neural) ectoderm goes on to form the outer skin covering. This whole process is called "neurulation" by embryologists, with the embryonic stage which succeeds the gastrula being called a "neurula". A mid-neurula is shown in relation to the earlier gastrulation movements in Fig. 16d (left). We recognize the brain and spinal cord primordia as a flat "neural plate", containing our marker 1, surrounded by folds. In a cross section through this stage (Fig. 16d, right) we find the marker in the middle of the neural plate (*NP*). Beneath the ectoderm

◄ Fig. 16a—d. Analysis of gastrulation movements according to the color marker method of W. Vogt. *Left:* external views. *Right:* sections. a Early gastrula with blastopore (*Bp*) and large blastocoel (continuation of Fig. 8). b Mid-gastrula with yolk plug (3), archenteron cavity (*AC*), roof of the archenteron (*AR*) and displaced blastocoel (*Bc*). c Late gastrula after completion of invagination of mesoderm and endoderm. d Locations of the color markers in the neurula: 1 in the neural plate (*N*), 2 in the notochord, 3 in the floor of the gut, 4 and 5 in the somites

lies the invaginated mesoderm of the archenteron roof. In the midline the cylindrical notochord has formed (marker 2) and separated from the lateral muscle primordia (markers 4 and 5). The borders of the mesoderm extending downward (lateral plate mesoderm, *LPM* in Fig. 15) will eventually surround the endoderm (3), in which the lumen of the gut is already visible.

Let us look at the formation of the nervous system a little more closely. At the cessation of gastrulation a shoe sole shaped area has formed on the dorsal surface of the embryo (a 1) (Fig. 17). Its borders (darkly stippled in the figure) soon enlarge into thickened folds (b 1). For the observer the plan of the future central nervous system becomes clearly discernible. The neural folds (*NF*) close over the neural plate (*NP*). The front part of this plate will form the brain (*B*); the rear part will form the spinal cord (*SC*). Skin ectoderm (*SkE*) forms the surface of the embryo covering the brain and the spinal cord.

Neurulation as a process of morphogenetic movements involves the reshaping of the neural plate into the neural tube. This occurs as the neural folds draw closer together and as, simultaneously, a groove forms in the neural plate (Fig. 17b); the neural folds ultimately meet and fuse in the midline. The skin ectoderm separates from the neural tube, an as it grows over it, submerges the closed neural tube within the embryo. Soon after, the parts, or vesicles, of the future brain (the telencephalon and diencephalon, which together make up the forebrain; the mesencephalon or midbrain; and the metencephalon and myelencephalon, comprising the hindbrain) become discernible as distinct swellings (Fig. 17c 1) molded from the neural tube. The eye cups will later bulge from the diencephalon (Fig. 25). The open space of the embryonic neural tube remains throughout life in the ventricles of the brain an in the central canal of the spinal cord.

At a later point (p. 108) we will take up the interesting question of the fate of the *neural crest* cells, those cells from the borders of the neural folds which are not incorporated into the neural tube.

We are not going to be satisfied, however, with a mere description of gastrulation, neurulation and organ formation. We want to understand the nature, causes and interrelationships of the morphogenetic processes. How are ordered cell movements directed and what decides which ectoderm cells are to form the epidermis and which to form the brain-spinal cord system? When does the fate of a given embryonic region become decided? When

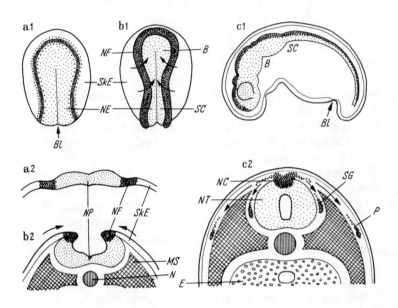

Fig. 17a—c. The processes of neurulation. Designations as in Fig. 15. *SkE* skin ectoderm (white); *NE* neural ectoderm and its derivatives (sparse dots); *NF* neural folds (black, dense dots); *MS* muscle segments (somites, cross-hatched); *N* notochord (vertically hatched); *E* gut endoderm (small circles). a 1 Early neurula with neural plate (*Bl* = site of the blastopore). a 2 Section through a 1 showing distribution of neural plate (*NP*) and neural fold material. b 1 Mid-neurula. b 2 Section through mid-neurula. c 1 Location of the submerged neural tube along the length of the embryo; *B* brain, *SC* spinal cord, *Bl* site of blastopore. c 2 Section through c 1 showing migration outward from the neural crest (*NC*) of cells destined to form spinal ganglia (*SG*) and pigment cells (*P*); *NT* neural tube

is it determined that a specific, unique path of differentiation will be followed? Questions of this sort call for intelligently conceived experiments and it is to the experimental analysis of development to which we now turn.

Toward Order and Pattern: Cells on the Move

The dramatic movements which produce an organism's richly diversified structures (Fig. 15c) from the simple hollow ball of the blastula (Fig. 11h) involve three distinguishable kinds of cell behavior: cell segregation, cell migration and cell association. These developmental dynamics begin with the segregation of the germ layers at gastrulation (p. 47). The cells destined to become ectoderm, mesoderm and endoderm move, not as individuals, but as members of cohesive units. The sheet of mesoderm migrates inward, involuting around the blastopore lip and coming to lie beneath the ectoderm where it forms the roof of the archenteron. The endoderm also disappears inside the embryo, becoming embedded in mesoderm, while the ectodermal sheet stretches to cover the whole embryo.

Cell segregation continues within the germ layers. The nervous system primordium separates from the skin ectoderm as the neural tube submerges into the embryo (Fig. 17). The mesoderm of the archenteron roof, which behaved at first as a uniform sheet of cells, also becomes divided up. The cylindrical notochord (Fig. 16d) forms in the midline as its cells segregate themselves from the neighboring mesoderm destined to form the skeleton and muscles of the trunk. In a similar way, the kidney tubules, blood vessels and gonad primordia arise as separate units.

In contrast to these movements of cell masses that subsequently are parcelled out into separate organ rudiments, development of the structures derived from the neural crest involves the migration of individual cells, often over impressive distances away from their original location (Figs. 17, 39). Some swarm outward to populate the skin of the entire organism, where they will differentiate into pigment cells. Other cells stream forth in close-order columns, moving downward to form the cartilage of the gill arches. Other cells move only a short distance: some form the mesenchyme inside the dorsal fin, while others associate in segmentally distributed groups alongside the neural tube, where they differentiate into the spinal ganglia (Figs. 17, 39).

Breaking down the description of morphogenetic cell movements into segregation, migration and association is somewhat arbitrary and artificial. For the analysis of these movements, however, it has the advantage that it helps us to dissect the problem into sub-questions more amenable to experimental approach.

Who gives the order to "move out"? What determines the path to be followed and what factors signal a cell to stop at the right place? What is it that impels cells in intimate contact suddenly to flee one another's company? How do migrating cells recognize others of their kind and, reassociating with them, come to rest at the proper place? We could easily go on with this list of questions, but there are already more than we shall be able to take up here. Only a few of the key experiments which have contributed most significantly to the clarification of these fundamental processes can be mentioned.

Situated next to one another in the amphibian neurula (Fig. 18a) are groups of cells whose developmental fate has already been determined. In our example (Fig. 18), a piece of embryo containing three cell types is excised (b) and placed in an alkaline culture medium where the cell mass loosens, releasing single cells (c) of all three types. These cells are mixed thoroughly to randomize the different cell types and are then placed in a conventional salt solution, one in which complete differentiation of tissue explants can later occur. The differently determined cells aggregate to form a sphere in which at first the various cell types are randomly distributed (Fig. 18d). This initial chaotic arrangement does not remain stable, however (Fig. 18e). Epidermal cells migrate outward and come to rest only when they have joined with other cells of their kind to form a continuous homogeneous outer layer. This reconstituted epidermal primordium differentiates into skin tissue. Avoiding any contact with the epidermal cells, the neural plate cells migrate inward until they have assembled themselves into a uniform central cell mass which will then develop further into a part of the spinal cord. Cells of the third type, those from the neural crest, take up positions between epidermis and spinal cord.

Through cell-type specific migration, segregation and association, a reorganization has been brought about in which the relative positions correspond closely to those observed for the same tissues during normal development (Fig. 18f). The structures which the excised piece would have formed are shown in Fig. 18g. At no place does the future spinal cord (neural tube, NT) have contact

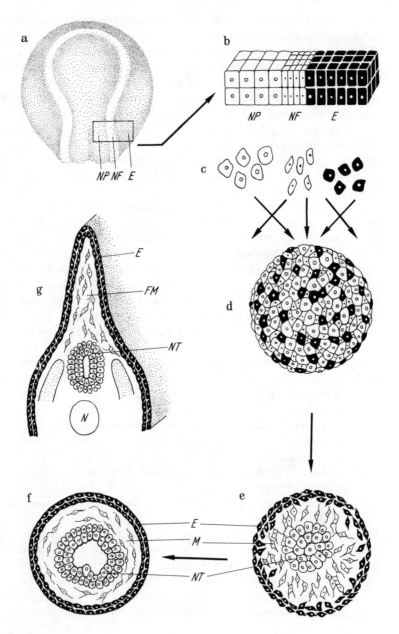

with the epidermis (E); filling the space between them are the neural crest-derived cells of the dorsal fin mesenchyme.

A comparable "sorting out" is obtained when skin ectoderm, mesoderm and endoderm cells are intermixed. Here, too, the different cell types resegregate. Movement continues until the ectoderm cells forming the skin primordium have assembled on the outside, the cells of mesodermal musculature or notochord primordium have assumed an intermediate position, and the gut-forming endoderm cells have located themselves at the center.

But can we now understand this kind of behavior which produces order out of chaos? There has been a continuing effort on the part of many researchers to clarify and explain this remarkable restructuring capability of dissociated cells.

Two factors seem to be involved—contact-dependent changes in cell motility and differential cell affinity. When they are removed from their usual contacts with their surroundings through explantation or dissociation there is a definite tendency for embryonic cells to begin movements. If pieces of two different tissues which normally have no mutual contact are apposed, there is a tendency for the two masses of heterotypic cells to spread apart and reduce their area of mutual contact. On the other hand, cells of the same kind have been observed to cease their movement when they come in contact with each other. This *contact inhibition* of the movement of isotypic cells presumably contributes to the stability of homogeneous tissue masses.

Many questions remain. Is sorting out of different cell types a result of positive affinity of isotypic cells, mutual repulsion (negative affinity) of heterotypic cells, or both? What is the nature of the factors responsible for differential cell affinity? Though nothing is known for certain, biochemical differences on the cell surface

---

◀ Fig. 18a—e. Re-establishment of order after dissociation and mixing of cells from an amphibian embryo. a Removal of a piece of ectoderm from a neurula. b The different cell types still segregated from one another. c Dissociated cells. d Random mixing of the three cell types is followed by reassociation into a sphere-shaped aggregate. e Re-segregation through cell movements. f Final arrangement, cell types in their natural order. g The part of the larva corresponding to the organized reaggregate in f. *NP* Cells of the neural plate, *NF* neural fold, *E* epidermis, *NT* neural tube, *M* mesenchyme, *FM* fin mesenchyme, *N* notochord. (Adapted from P. L. Townes and J. Holtfreter)

are probably the most important factors responsible for the sorting out of heterotypic cells. Also unsolved is the question whether selective cell association depends upon mutual recognition of cell type-specific surface components, or whether sorting out is the result only of quantitative differences in some general adhesive property of cells. The latter mechanism would explain the fact that in experiments involving sorting out of two types of cells, one type always winds up on the inside while the other always moves to the periphery, since for two cell types of different adhesiveness, the most stable arrangement would have the more adhesive cells in the middle of the ball, enveloped by the less adhesive ones. However, direct measurements of differences in cell adhesiveness to support this theory of sorting out are lacking, and, in any case, additional involvement of specific recognition factors will be difficult to exclude. If such mutual recognition does occur, the recognition factors involved must be tissue-specific, not species-specific. This was shown with mixtures of future kidney and cartilage cells from chick and mouse embryos. The tissue masses are gently "loosened" by the action of the digestive enzyme trypsin, releasing individual cells into the culture medium, where they remain dissociated for only a short time before aggregating into mixed cell clumps. The kidney cells of chick and mouse adhere closely and collaborate in constructing chimeric kidney tubules. The cartilage-forming cells of these two unrelated donors also associate into a cohesive cell mass comprised partly of chick and partly of mouse cells. In heterotypic combinations, on the other hand, sorting out does occur. Chick kidney cells separate from mouse cartilage cells, just as they segregate from chick cartilage cells. Mouse kidney cells also segregate from chick cartilage cells.

So far the discussion has concerned only cell-cell interactions involving direct contact. Cases are also known, however, in which cells influence one another over a distance. In the newt embryo, propigment cells derived from the neural crest (p. 108) migrate over long distances, eventually populating the entire skin of the larva, where they then become pigmented. A striking feature of these pigment cells is the way they are scattered so that they tend to maintain a certain minimum separation from one another (Figs. 5, 33, 34). It looks as if they are mutually repulsing one another, and indeed such a reaction can be shown experimentally. If a single propigment cell is placed in a fine glass tube it will hardly move (Fig. 19a). If, on the other hand, two or more cells are isolated and placed together in the capillary, they soon move away from one another until a considerable distance between them has been established (Fig. 19b). Evidently they are able

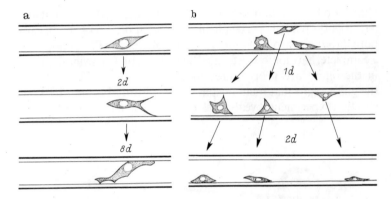

Fig. 19a and b. Negative chemotaxis in propigment cells of a newt. a A single cell hardly changes its position even after 8 days (8d) in culture. b Behavior of a group of three cells cultured together. *Top:* after several hours in culture; *middle:* after 1 day (1d); *bottom:* after 2 days (2d). (After V. C. Twitty and M. C. Niu)

to react to substances which diffuse from individual cells into the environment by migrating away from those regions where the concentration of the substances is the highest. This experiment makes understandable the pattern of pigment cells in the intact larva and draws our attention to one of the few known cases in which the cells of a higher organism respond to the presence of a chemical substance with directed movements. The *negative chemotaxis* of the propigment cells, in which they strive to get away from one another, stands in contrast to the more usual tendency of like cells to associate, as shown in Fig. 18.

The analysis of differential cell affinities has revealed important underlying features of the morphogenetic dynamics that shape the developing organism. Still, many of the questions raised in this chapter remain unanswered. Further progress in this area will undoubtedly depend in large measure upon advances in our knowledge of the chemical properties and structural features of cell surface membranes.

Experimental Production of Identical Twins

Hair loop constriction of a late newt blastula, provided that the constriction plane is perpendicular to the upper lip of the blastopore, produces two half-embryos, each of which will develop into a complete, harmoniously formed newt (Fig. 20). The twins depicted in the figure are nearly three months old; the reduced size of the gills signals that metamorphosis has already begun. This constriction experiment reveals an astonishing and fascinating capabil-

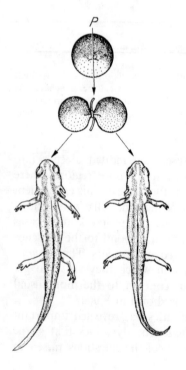

Fig. 20. Complete regulative development in both halves after constriction of a late blastula of the newt *Triturus taeniatus*. *P* plane of symmetry; the area above the future blastopore (slit) is darkly pigmented. (After H. Spemann and H. Falkenberg)

ity of the developing organism. How does this happen? Had there been no experimental intervention, the cells of either side of the embryo would have formed only one side of the newt's body, with only one eye and a single foreleg and hindleg. But after the constriction, a completely new disposition of the available cell material occurs. The old blueprint (Fig. 15) has to be scrapped. Totally revised construction plans have to be introduced, including a new median axis, providing also for a general reduction in scale. Shortage of building materials means that, for the time being, everything, including eyes and brain, gut and heart, must be built only half as large as had been originally planned. Later on, after the larvae have begun to feed, however, they attain a normal body size.

The ability of isolated parts of the developing organism to adopt a new plan, reorganize accordingly and go on to complete construction of a whole organism, has been called "regulation" or, to avoid confusion, "regulative development". Human identical twins owe their existence and normal harmonious development to this same regulative capacity. At some early stage, during cleavage of perhaps even later, the embryo must have "fallen apart" so that the inherent regulative capacity could come into play. Whether the causes of the separation are chemical, mechanical, or some combination of these two is unknown. The human capacity for regulative development was impressively shown by the Dionne quintuplets of Canada. These five girls, who grew up into normal individuals, began life as a single biological entity.

Let us now see what happens when we divide an amphibian embryo in two by constriction at a still later stage, after completion of gastrulation. Once again we align the loop along the midline and draw it tight. And once again the separated parts go on to develop further, but now they can no longer "regulate" completely. The animals that form are one-sided defectives possessing only a single eye and missing both legs on one side or the other. In this case the isolated half produces essentially only those structures which it would have formed in the intact embryo in the absence of constriction. Something crucial has evidently happened in the course of gastrulation, obliterating the far-reaching regulative capacity of the younger embryo. How this restrictive transformation occurs can only be revealed through further experiments.

59

Exchanging Future Skin and Brain Cells

Hans Spemann was the first to show how marvelously the embryos of the Amphibia lend themselves to surgical operations. Using homemade microsurgical instruments, such as glass needles, pipettes and hair loops, he could dissect out a piece from any region of a blastula or gastrula and then transplant it wherever he chose, either elsewhere in the same embryo or into a different one. The manipulations are performed under a binocular dissecting microscope which magnifies the pinhead-sized egg so much that, with a proper amount of practice, the experimenter gets the feeling he's operating on a basketball. The embryos can tolerate radical surgery, and even the biggest transplanted pieces heal into place within a quarter of an hour. Once sulfa drugs and antibiotics became available, the danger of infection was overcome, and now large series of operated animals are routinely kept in culture to any desired stage.

Since one wants to be able to trace the fate of a group of transplanted cells, they must be marked in some way. For his experiments Spemann used embryos which differed in their natural pigmentation. Taking a light-colored embryo as donor and a dark-colored one as host, he was able to keep the lighter cells under constant observation and even to recognize them later in microscopic sections. Nowadays either donor or host is simply stained a bright blue-green with the harmless vital dye, nile blue sulfate. For many weeks thereafter the border between implant and host remains precisely delineated down to the last cell.

Having thus mentioned a few technical points, let us turn now to a classical experiment, published by Spemann in 1918, which clarified one of the fundamental questions of developmental biology (Fig. 21).

Pieces of ectoderm are exchanged between two embryos which have just begun gastrulation (a1 and b1). From their positions with respect to the blastopore (curved arrow) we know that the dark piece comes from the future brain region, while the light piece would have formed the epidermis of the belly. As a result of the transplantation, cells which normally would have formed brain come to lie in the skin primordium and skin ectoderm cells now find themselves located in the brain-forming region.

The transplants adapt completely to their new surroundings—the "brain" cells remain on the surface, spread out smoothly along with the rest of the epidermis, and, aside from their darker pigmen-

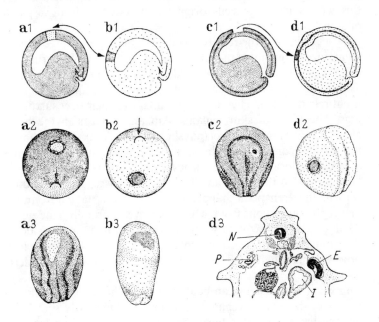

Fig. 21a—d. H. Spemann's classical exchange transplant experiments on newt embryos, performed either at the beginning (a and b) or after completion of gastrulation. a1 and b1 Diagram of the operation whereby neural ectoderm from a1 (dark) is exchanged with skin ectoderm from b1 (light). The arrow within the dorsal blastopore lip indicates the direction of invagination. a2 and b2 Location of the newly implanted pieces in relation to the blastopore (arrow). a3 Implant is located in the brain part of the neural plate (cf. Fig. 14). b3 The other implant is located in the ectoderm on the underside of the head. c1 and c2 Donor of neural material (gap). d1 and d2 Host neurula with implant taken from c in its flank. d3 Further development of the larva (section). Implant develops into an eye (E). Host organs: N neural tube, P pronephros, I intestine

tation, cannot be distinguished from their neighbors in the adjacent epidermis (b3, Fig. 21). The former "skin" cells, too, fulfill in every respect the demands of their new location (a3). They participate in the construction of that part of the brain appropriate to the occupied site and differentiate into proper nerve cells. The same newt will later control movements and process sensory information, perform instinctive actions and learn from experiences—all this with a group of cells originally destined to form a patch of skin.

Now let us look at the results of a corresponding exchange experiment, carried out not at the beginning but at the end of gastrulation (Figs. 21 c, 21 d). The transplanted pieces look just as embryonic as those of the first experiment, and yet their subsequent behavior is entirely different. They no longer adapt to their new surroundings. The piece of skin remains skin and persists in the brain as a disruptive foreign object (not shown). The chunk of brain-forming tissue separates from the surrounding skin and differentiates at the new location into whichever part of the brain it would have formed at the site from which it was excised. In the example shown, the transplant happens to have been taken from the diencephalon region, from which the eyes normally emerge (p. 73, Fig. 25). Consequently, the implant located in the side of the animal develops into an isolated eye, an eye lacking a lens, however, since there is no longer any contact with the skin ectoderm (cf. p. 75).

Important conclusions can be drawn from the radically different results of these two exchange experiments. Obviously something decisive has happened to the embryonic ectoderm during gastrulation. In the early gastrula cells still have the potential to become either skin or brain. They are not yet "*determined*", and so, when transplanted, they conform to local "ground rules". Their differentiation is *dependent* on the surroundings. At the end of gastrulation, on the other hand, "*determination*" is complete. The once extensive repertoire of developmental possibilities has become reduced to a single organ system. Now the transplants "do their own thing", no longer going along with the locally prevailing behavior pattern. They "self-differentiate" *independent* of influences from the surroundings.

By using the various italicized expressions just now we have introduced some of the technical language of developmental biologists originally adopted because of the need to understand and explain transplantation experiments on amphibians.

The "Organizer"

We now know that the developmental fate of many cell regions and organ primordia is decided during gastrulation. As one example of this, ectoderm becomes determined to make either nervous system or skin. We are naturally interested to know

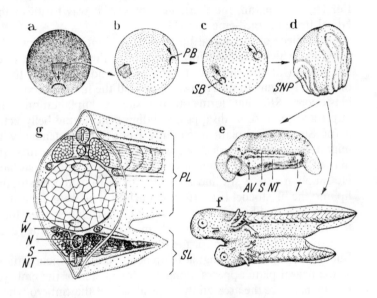

Fig. 22a—g. Transplantation of the "organizer". a Dark-colored donor, from which a piece of tissue lying above the sickle-shaped blastopore is removed for implantation into another embryo. b Light-colored host embryo with darkly pigmented implant in the belly ectoderm; *PB* primary blastopore of the host with arrow showing direction of migration at beginning of invagination. c Implant invaginates around lip of secondary blastopore (*SB*). d Primary neural plate (larger, right) and secondary neural plate (*SNP*) above the implant. e Induction of auditory vesicles (*AV*), neural tube (*NT*), somites (*S*) and tail bud (*T*) on the left side of the host. f Complete secondary embryo representing maximal inductive effect of the "organizer". g Section through f shows the primary larval organs (*PL*) above and the organization of the secondary larva (*SL*) below, with the implant cells shown dark and the host cells light; *NT* neural tube, *S* somites, *N* notochord, *W* Wolffian duct, *I* intestinal lumen. (Adapted in part from H. Spemann and J. Holtfreter)

whether further experimentation can reveal anything of the causal factors underlying these processes.

Having shown that ectodermal transplants in early gastrulae adapt themselves to their new locations and differentiate accordingly, Spemann and his co-workers decided to try transplanting, at the same early stage, pieces of mesoderm taken from the dorsal lip of the blastopore (Fig. 22). A seemingly harmless experiment and yet it led to one of the greatest discoveries ever in the life sciences. For Hans Spemann, the German zoologist, it was to mean the Nobel Prize for medicine in 1935.

When a piece of the dorsal lip (Fig. 22a) is introduced into the ectoderm which later will form the skin of the belly (b), it does not remain at the surface. It behaves instead according to its origin and begins to move inward, around the lip of a secondary blastopore (SB) that forms at the site of implantation. The implanted piece soon disappears, sliding beneath the belly ectoderm. Since the implant apparently has a built-in tendency to migrate beneath the surface anyway, the experimenter can spare himself the trouble of fitting it carefully into the embryo surface. He simply makes a slit and sticks the piece from the blastopore lip into the blastocoel (Fig. 16, Bl), much as if he were depositing a letter in a mailbox. The movements of gastrulation then force the implant against the belly ectoderm, leading to the same result as a superficial transplant of the type shown in Fig. 22.

But the really astonishing development occurs at neurulation, as the neural plate appears along the dorsal side of the embryo. For then, above the area on the ventral side of the embryo where the piece of mesoderm lies buried, a second neural plate appears. Like its dorsal counterpart, this structure will later close over, resulting in a second, abdominal, neural tube. And, let us not forget, a secondary nervous system like this is formed from ecto-dermal cells that normally would have made only skin!

This unexpected developmental performance was forced upon the ectoderm by the underlying implant. The implant functions as "inducer"; it *induces* the skin ectoderm of the belly to make a neural plate. In favorable cases implantation results not just in a secondary neural plate, but in a whole secondary embryo, with head, eyes, balancers, gills, ears, somites, notochord, pronephros and gut (Fig. 22f and g). The implant exerts a powerful influence on surrounding host cells, resulting in the formation of combined structures derived partly from implant cells and partly from host cells. In a cross section of an induced secondary embryo (Fig. 22 g) we see that both the notochord and the somites are combinations of implant cells (dark) and host cells (light). The mesodermal implant has additionally provided a sector of the neural tube; involved here are a few cells that remained on the surface during gastrulation. This formation of harmoniously integrated, combined structures is evidence that we are dealing with more than the mere triggering of host neural ectoderm development by the implanted dorsal lip, as implied by the term "inducer". Spemann preferred to speak of the "organization center" or "organizer". For the following experiments concerning the origin and role of this region in normal development we can retain Spemann's terminology. After discussing further experiments dealing with its mechanism of action, however, we shall be forced to reconsider this matter.

It has been established through numerous experiments that the "organization center" corresponds to the region of the blastula lying above the site of the blastopore which, after migrating inward during gastrulation to form the mesoderm of the archenteron roof, eventually produces mainly notochord and somites. The organizer region itself is determined much earlier, however. A specific area of the egg cortex has been identified in the still unfertilized oocyte of the clawed frog *(Xenopus laevis)*. This area becomes visible after fertilization as the "gray crescent". Irradiation of this area with ultraviolet light results in defective development: no nervous system is formed in the damaged embryo. This experiment tells us that even in the cytoplasm of the maturing egg, i.e. prior to fertilization, the cortical layer must be arranged in a kind of mosaic, with the organizer region fixed at a specific location.

The cells which receive this special cytoplasm during cleavage later lie above the site of the blastopore and migrate inward to form the archenteron roof. Something crucial for the future organizer is evidently formed in the egg cell under the influence of the maternal genes. We have already discussed in some detail the problem of gene action before fertilization (p. 23).

It should be emphasized that organizer implants frequently induce only partial embryos. Thus, the embryo shown in Fig. 22e is lacking the front part of its head. Here the secondary embryo primordium extended only as far as the auditory vesicles (*AV*). Now that we know that a piece of organizer implanted into the future abdomen or flank region can induce an additional embryo primordium, the question comes up whether an organizer function is also required in normal development. There are various kinds of experiments which provide an answer to this. One can, for example, constrict the embryo with a hair loop in such a way that only one of the halves gets the organizer (Fig. 23a). The result is unambiguous: only the half with the organizer cells is able to regulate and develop into a normal larva (b). The other looped-off half doesn't die, however; it lives on for weeks,

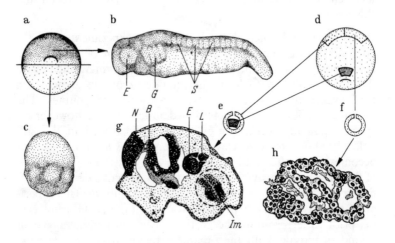

Fig. 23a—h. Indispensability of the "organizer" material. a Early gastrula is sectioned into upper and lower halves (line). b Entire organism derived from the upper half; *E* eye, *G* gills, *S* somites. c Vegetal fragment (amorphous embryo) from the lower half. d Donor embryo provides not yet determined neural ectoderm (sparsely dotted) and "organizer" cells (densely dotted). e and f Ectoderm sandwiches with and without filling of organizer material. g The filling (implant *Im*, dashed circle) induced in the ectoderm an eye (*E*) with lens (*L*), as well as brain (*B*) and nose (*N*). h Explanted ectoderm alone produces only an atypical epidermis. (After H. Spemann and J. Holtfreter)

but merely produces a shapeless mass (c) comprised of yolk-rich endoderm cells and a covering of skin. These "vegetal fragments" are missing all axial organs, and, in particular, lack the primordium for a nervous system.

We showed earlier (Fig. 20) that harmoniously formed identical twins can arise from halved newt embryos. Such regulative achievements are obviously only possible if both halves are furnished with a sufficient fraction of the organization center. An even distribution of organizer material is also a prerequisite in the case of human identical twins. Should this fail to be achieved, only one embryo develops normally while the other remains a misshapen vegetal fragment. Occasionally such "amorphous fetuses" are carried to full term and are born along with the normal twin.

The indispensable role of the archenteron roof in the formation of the nervous tissue can be seen from the results of the so-called "sandwich experiment" (Fig. 23d—h), which was designed to rule out possible influences of other regions of the embryo. If a piece of early gastrula ectoderm is removed from the area of the future brain and spinal cord and placed in a salt solution of appropriate concentration, it rapidly rounds up into a vesicle (f). This "explant" will go on to produce only an atypical sort of epidermis (h). Although the explanted material in the depicted experiment was taken from the future neural ectoderm, neither spinal cord nor brain develops from it. Some exceptions to this rule will be discussed later (p. 70).

If a cell clump is now taken from the dorsal lip of the blastopore and placed on another flattened-out piece of ectoderm, the ectoderm will enclose the organizer cells (e) as it rounds up. And, as a result of induction by the sandwich filling, the same ectoderm which otherwise made only skin now develops into parts of numerous organs, such as brain, eyes, ears, balancers, spinal cord, muscle, and kidney. Pigment cells appear, too. This demonstrates once more that the nervous system does not form in the absence of induction. There is ample evidence, then, that the organizer really has an indispensable function in normal development.

Looking back to experiments discussed earlier, we realize that certain results become understandable only now. During gastrulation the invaginating mesoderm of the archenteron roof comes to underlie a part of the ectoderm. This ectodermal area, as a result of inductive influences emanating from the underlying archenteron roof, becomes "determined" to form nervous tissue, while the remaining ectoderm, lacking such stimulus, goes on to make epidermis. This determination does not occur until the gastrulation movements have brought close surface-to-surface contacts between the "organizer" and the future neural tissue. Now we can also understand the ectoderm transplant experiments: why pieces of ectoderm, if transplanted before gastrulation, behave in keeping with their new surroundings, yet if transplanted after the invagination of the archenteron differentiate according to their place of origin.

On the Mechanism of Embryonic Induction

Ever since Spemann's discoveries at the beginning of the 'twenties, a great number of researchers have concerned themselves with the process of induction, carrying out countless experiments. Despite this intensive, many-sided research effort, many important questions remain unanswered. Developmental biologists have termed the 'twenties the "Period of Hope", the next decade the "Period of Confusion", and the 'forties the "Period of Depression". The years since 1950 are perhaps a "Period of Renewed Hope". Let us now recount some of the things that have been clarified in the course of all these ups and downs.

If the archenteron roof from a frog or toad is implanted into a newt embryo it has exactly the same inductive effect as in its own species. This lack of species specificity even holds true over much wider degrees of kinship: an additional embryo primordium can be induced in the embryonic shield of a chick with "organizer" material from amphibia, fish or mammals. Evidently the active principle is the same for all vertebrates—determination of the nervous system must be everywhere based on the same mechanisms.

An illuminating parallel to this exists: many hormones are known to act, within wide boundaries, with a similar lack of species specificity. If calf thyroid glands are fed to tadpoles, they trigger metamorphosis just as well as the frog's own thyroid. And a rooster's comb will respond to any male sex hormone, regardless of whether it is from a fish or a man. This broad action spectrum of the hormones depends on the fact that the thyroids, adrenals and gonads produce and release into the blood identical or very similar compounds in all the vertebrates. But before we can carry the parallel any further we have to prove that substances emanating from the archenteron roof penetrate the superimposed ectoderm and that, once there, they induce the formation of a nervous system. For all we know at this point, the "organizer" could be functioning by means of a radiation field or, indeed, through some sort of mysterious "vital force".

What is the evidence that chemical substances indispensable for neural ectoderm determination are transferred from the archenteron roof to the ectoderm? One approach is to block the normal contact between inducer and ectoderm. If a thin, poreless, membrane is slipped between the two tissues, no induction takes place. If, however, this membrane is replaced by a Millipore filter, 20 microns (thousandths of a millimeter) thick with tiny pores only 0.8 micron in diameter, induction will ensue. Such "transfilter induction" has generally been taken as evidence that direct cell-to-cell contact is not necessary in normal induction. However, recent electron micrographs of filters used in transfilter experiments show that cell extensions can penetrate deep into the pores of the filter, approaching and possibly contacting similar extensions of cells from the other side. Transfilter experiments thus do not absolutely rule out the need for surface-to-surface cell contact in normal induction.

There are, however, other findings which do speak against the need for direct contact. Pieces of the archenteron roof can retain their inductive capacity even after the cells have been rendered non-viable by various treatments (heating, cold, certain chemicals). Inductive substances can be extracted from all kinds of sources. When agar cubes impregnated with these substances are implanted into young amphibian embryos they induce neural development in a manner similar to living inducer tissues.

But what kinds of substances are these which have been given such an important function in embryonic development? Despite decades of effort and experimentation of the most varied kinds, this question has never been satisfactorily answered. It has been possible to elicit quite convincing inductions with pure substances

69

from the chemical shelf. Among the effective substances were fatty acids, steroids, carbohydrates, vitamins, and nucleic acids, as well as various proteins. Now one doesn't know whether the factors responsible for normal induction are represented among these substances. It also remains open whether or not these diverse substances all have a direct effect. Some of them could be influencing various metabolic processes. Modifications in cell chemistry could lead to production of other, unknown, substances capable of affecting neural determination directly. Furthermore, isolated skin ectoderm from a blastula has the tendency when damaged to develop into nervous tissue without the need for action of any inducer. Thus, the inductive effects of chemical compounds could result, in many cases, from a simple damaging of the target system. For all these reasons the authorities in this area of research have been unable to agree about the chemical nature of the naturally occurring inducer substances. And making things somewhat more difficult to analyze is the probability that more than one inducer substance is given off by the archenteron roof. How do we come to this conclusion?

We know that the brain primordium is found above the anterior, or front, part of the archenteron roof, while the spinal cord develops above the posterior, or rear, part. Where a secondary embryo is induced, the anterior-posterior differences encompass other organ systems as well. How do such regional differences originate? Is there a "head inducer" distinguishable from a "back-rump-tail inducer" or do the anterior-posterior differences in differentiation depend on the properties of the reacting material itself? If so, during normal development the ectoderm would have to bring about its own pattern of differentiation, with the underlying archenteron roof giving a single inductive order: "nervous tissue". It is possible to distinguish between these alternatives experimentally. Two different types of sandwich were assembled (Fig. 24); the ectoderm on the outside has to be the same in both cases (a 1 and a 2), so undifferentiated ectoderm from an early gastrula is used. In the first experiment (c) a piece of anterior archenteron roof is taken as sandwich filling; in the second (d) the "meat" of the sandwich is a piece of tissue taken from the posterior part of the archenteron roof. As Fig. 24 shows, the first piece induces a wide variety of head structures (e), while identical ecto-

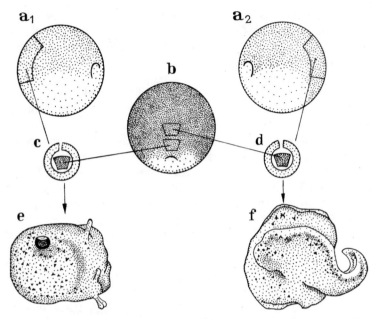

Fig. 24a—f. Specificity of inductive actions from different regions of the organization center. a1 and a2 Early newt gastrulae as sources of ectoderm. b Early toad gastrula *(Bombina)* as source of organizer material for sandwich fillings. c and d Cells destined to form anterior (c) and posterior (d) archenteron roof. e Induction of head organs (eye and balancers visible). f Induction of rump-tail organs (spinal cord, muscle, fin). (Adapted from J. Holtfreter)

derm reacts in the second experiment by forming structures typical of the rump and tail regions (f).

The pattern of development in the ectoderm-derived structures is thus not (or not only) brought about by qualities inherent to the reacting system, but rather by differences in the inductive signals put forth by different parts of the archenteron roof. This is the best evidence available that the archenteron roof is truly an "organization center", with region-specific differences in inducer activity. And since, as we will see, these differences must be chemical, we again face the question of the specific nature of the substances involved. We now have evidence that there are distinct "head" and "back" inducers. What can we learn about these substances?

Some progress was made with pieces of various tissues taken from adult guinea pigs and implanted beneath the not-yet-determined amphibian ectoderm. Liver induced head organs, primarily forebrain, while bone marrow was effective as a notochord-muscle inducer, with much of the muscle being provided by the overlying ectoderm. Experiments with tissues of adult birds, fish, newts and mice led to similar results. The advantage of using non-amphibian sources is that they often provide a more suitable material for large scale extraction and purification of the active substance(s). To follow the course of purification of the active material, agar cubes could be impregnated with extract fractions and tested for activity by implantation. Recently, it has been possible using a tedious multistep procedure to isolate in pure form one milligram of an active protein from one kilogram of young chick embryos. In the amphibian embryo this protein induces mesodermal organs such as musculature and notochord of the rump-tail region.

Proteins are probably also crucial for the induction of the anterior parts of the head, though lately there is a tendency to think that these proteins must first form a complex with ribonucleic acid (RNA) molecules before they can become active. Between the forebrain and spinal cord region lies the area of the hindbrain. Certain experiments have led to the conclusion that in this "no man's land" the head and back-rump-tail inducers are active together. A gradient of a "rump-tail inducer" declining towards the front of the animal would overlap a gradient of "forebrain inducer" dropping off towards the rear. And in the intermediate overlap zone the specific structures of the hindbrain region would be induced.

A lot more research will have to be done to work out the chemistry of the different inducer substances. And yet, even when that aspect is cleared up, the hard-to-fathom problem of how these substances act will remain unsolved. How is it that embryonic cells can react differently to stimuli of different kinds, forming eye in response to one stimulus and muscle in response to another? Apparently different inducing substances activate different sets of genes, "turning on" the "eye program" in one case and the "muscle program" in another. But the developmental biology of our day has hardly begun to scratch the surface of such goings-on.

Before the discussion is extended to other examples of embryonic induction (see following chapter), our use of the term "organizer" should be reconsidered. The embryonic area above the dorsal lip of the blastopore, which later becomes the roof of the archenteron, certainly plays a dominant role in development. No normal embryonic organization is initiated in its absence (p. 66). Moreover, chemical signals from different regions of the "organization center" influence such general qualities as head *versus* tail. But does the "organizer" really *organize* cells derived from various sources into the harmoniously structured secondary embryo? We must be careful not to ascribe too much to the "organizer". In all likelihood, it sends forth a limited number of relatively simple substances which serve merely as triggers of "self-organization" in the reacting tissues.

We have already dealt in an earlier chapter (p. 52) with the kinds of processes which are involved in the *self-assembly* or *self-organization* of cells into tissues and organs. The cells of embryonic blastemas, such as germ layers, are provided with an inherent and autonomous capacity for segregation into organ primordia. Interactions among developing tissues and organs lead to a mutual equilibrium of properly proportioned structures. The "organizer" is just a region of the embryo endowed with those inductive capabilities that set in motion the whole sequence of interactions through which the genetic blueprint is made a reality.

Lens Induction and Hierarchy of Inducers

Formation of the vertebrate eye involves the joining together of different elements that initially were completely separated from one another. We see in Fig. 25a that the cells of the future optic cup lie in the brain part of the neural plate while the lens is derived from an area of skin ectoderm lying at some distance. How do these two primordia get together?

After the neural tube has formed, paired optic vesicles (*OC* in Fig. 25b) begin to bulge out laterally from the diencephalon (posterior part of the forebrain) eventually touching the skin ectoderm (*L*). Next the simple optic vesicle becomes indented, forming the double-walled optic cup (c). The thicker layer lining the cup will

73

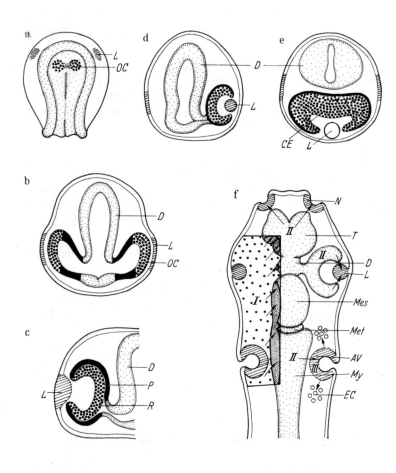

Fig. 25a—f. Eye development, lens induction and hierarchy of inducers. a Position of the future optic cup (*OC*) material and of the lens ectoderm (*L*) in the neurula. b Later, optic cups (*OC*) bulge out laterally from the diencephalon (*D*). c Newly formed optic cup consisting of retina (*R*) and pigment layer (*P*) has induced lens (*L*). d No lens forms on left after removal of optic cup (lens ectoderm diagonally hatched). e Cyclopean eye (*CE*) induces lens in abnormal location. f Diagram of inductive interactions in the head region. I. Archenteron roof (large dots) induces brain formation: *T* telencephalon, *D* diencephalon with optic cups, *Mes* mesencephalon, *Met* metencephalon, *My* myelencephalon. II. Parts of brain (fine dots) induce nose (*N*), lens (*L*) and auditory vesicles (*AV*) (all three diagonally hatched). III. Auditory vesicle induces the cartilaginous ear capsule *EC*. (e after H. B. Adelmann)

become the retina (R) while the cells of the outer wall will form the pigment layer (P). Where the rim of this optic cup pushes against the skin the epidermis thickens into the lens primordium (L). This cell mass then detaches itself from its place of origin and settles into the pupil opening of the optic cup, where it differentiates into the transparent lens (L in d and e).

The investigator, concerned as he is with cause and effect, would now like to know whether the lens self-differentiates or whether its formation is perhaps induced by the optic cup. Experiments with many vertebrates have shown that if an embryonic optic cup is removed soon enough, no lens will develop on that side of the animal, although the lens-forming material remains intact (diagonal hatching in Fig. 25d, left). If, on the other hand, the area which normally becomes lens is replaced with flank epidermis, the "alien" cells now located at the surface above the optic cup react by forming a lens. Finally, an optic cup transplanted beneath the skin of flank or belly is capable of inducing a proper lens in that strange location.

Further information along the same lines comes from certain cases of abnormal development in which only a single eye forms in the middle of the forehead. In a cyclops of this kind the anterior part of the archenteron roof may be poorly developed or damaged; therefore a weakened diencephalon can result. And now, instead of a pair of laterally protruding optic vesicles, a single medial optic cup is formed (Figs. 25e and 28f). This cyclopean eye induces a lens in a place where none would form otherwise, while the lateral lens ectoderm now develops into ordinary skin.

Various experimental approaches thus provide more than adequate proof that the optic cup functions as inducer of the lens. And yet, quite remarkably, there are several amphibians—including the European water frog—in which the lens can differentiate in the absence of the optic cup, that is, the lens appears to form without any inducer.

This apparent contradiction was a stimulus to further research. It turns out that we have oversimplified the process of lens induction in our initial presentation. Recent experiments have shown that there are three overlapping stages in the overall process, in which three distinct interacting systems take part. First, in the early gastrula while the two primordia are in contact the

75

endodermal wall of the foregut has an inducing effect on the future lens epidermis. In the second phase, i.e. in late gastrula, this influence is reinforced by the heart mesoderm which now touches the lens-forming region. Only after the eye cups have formed following neurulation does the classical lens induction by the retinal layer of the optic cup come into play. The effects of these three sets of tissue interactions are additive; the three phases reinforce one another. It is quite possible, therefore, that the first two phases are sufficient in the case of the water frog. Multi-step inductions have also been demonstrated in the formation of the nose and in the development of the auditory vesicles. Moreover, we now know that the induced organ can in many cases act back upon its own inducer. Thus the developing lens exerts an effect upon the cellular organization of the retina, which meanwhile, of course, has been developing from part of the lens-inducing optic cup. It is this interplay, this give-and-take, which ensures harmonious development of an integrated organism.

Now we are ready to place the inductive interaction optic cup-lens within a still larger and more general scheme of things. The optic cup is nothing else but an outwardly displaced part of the embryonic diencephalon. It owes its existence to the inductive activity of the archenteron roof. Without this primary inducer there would be no brain (p. 82), and hence no eyes. When the optic cup subsequently brings about the formation of a lens it does so as a secondary inducer, since it itself is the "product" of the primary inducer. Other parts of the brain also act as secondary inducers (Fig. 25f). The forebrain induces nose formation, while influences from the hindbrain induce the auditory vesicles in the overlying skin. The auditory vesicle develops into the soft labyrinth of the inner ear, which in turn acts as a tertiary inducer, promoting formation of the cartilaginous ear capsule from the surrounding cells. Finally, it has been established that development of the tympanic membrane results from an inductive stimulus of the fourth order originating in the ear capsule. Hierarchically regulated sequences of inductive interactions, with each successive inducer owing its existence to the one before, guide the development in space and time of organ primordia in the embryo. As understanding of the mechanisms and complexities of embryonic induction has gradually deepened over the years, developmental biologists have increasingly avoided the use of terms such as "the organizer" or "the lens inducer" which seem to have a unidirectional, once-and-for-all quality about them. The tendency today is to speak of "inductive interactions".

A Newt with a Frog's Mouth

Though freshly hatched amphibian larvae still possess no legs to grasp with, they nevertheless are able to stabilize themselves by holding fast to nearby objects. The tadpoles of anurans (tailless or frog-like amphibians) can anchor themselves to plants, rocks or even the film on the water's surface with the aid of an adhesive secretion from a pair of bowl-shaped suckers (S, Fig. 26b). In the larvae of the urodeles (tailed amphibians) this attachment function is performed by slender balancers (B, Fig. 26a). These early larval grasping organs regress later on, after the limbs have sprouted forth.

In newts and salamanders the larval mouth is endowed early on with a set of genuine, hard, bony teeth (T). By contrast, frog

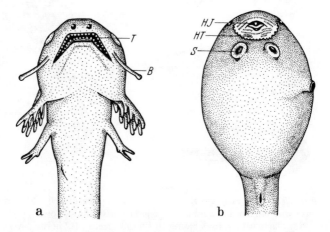

Fig. 26a and b. Mouth armament and adhesive organs in a tailed amphibians (newt) and b tailless amphibians (frog tadpole). T (true) teeth, B balancer, HT horny "teeth", HJ horny jaws, S sucker

and toad tadpoles are armed only with epidermal horny jaws (*HJ*) and horny teeth (*HT*) arranged in characteristic rows.

The experimenter would naturally like to learn something of the fundamental developmental dynamics which lead to such diverse grasping organs and mouth armaments. A particularly informative experimental approach is depicted in Fig. 27. A piece of future belly, flank or back epidermis is excised from the early gastrula (a) of either a frog *(Rana)* or a toad *(Bombina)*, and then implanted in the future mouth region of a newt embryo (b). Two questions are of immediate interest: Is the translocated piece even capable of forming mouth structures? And if it is, are the mouth parts that form frog-specific or newt-specific or some compromise between the two? The result is unambiguous. Fig. 27c shows a robust newt larva in which the mouth region is occupied by a frog ectoderm implant. We see that a typical tadpole mouth has formed, with horny jaws (*HJ*), slender horny teeth (*HT*),

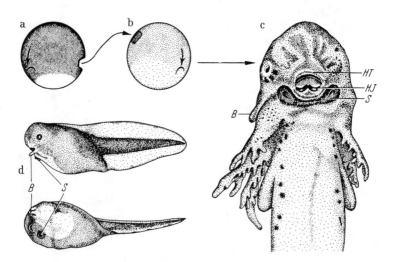

Fig. 27a—d. a Frog gastrula as donor of a piece of belly ectoderm. b Newt host with implant in future mouth region; arrow shows dorsal lip of blastopore. c Newt larva with a frog's mouth (*HT* horny "teeth", *HJ* horny jaws) and suckers (*S*); *B* balancer of the newt larva. d Toad larva *(Bombina)* with a light-colored implant from a newt embryo. Implant has formed balancer (*B*), toad has formed sucker (*S*). (c after E. Rotmann; d after O. Schotté)

and large suckers (*S*). In addition, the balancer is missing on the left side, while on the right side this typical newt organ does appear, in a region not occupied by the implant (*B*).

If the roles of donor and host are reversed a corresponding result is obtained. In Fig. 27d we have a drawing of a toad larva which has a newt balancer (*B*) sticking out from the region of the implant. If the implanted newt cells had also covered the mouth region, true bony teeth would have formed in place of the toad's horny mouth parts.

Let us now try to analyze these remarkable developmental accomplishments. First, we have the fact that transplanted belly epidermis can react to inductive stimuli in a way that corresponds to its new surroundings, by forming mouth parts and grasping organs. We have already noted that inducers can be effective far beyond their own species borders (p. 68). And yet it has to amaze us that the frog or toad skin is able to understand so well the construction orders coming from the newt host. The second point is that in carrying out the transmitted job order the frog implant remains true to the species from which it came. The order "mouth parts" is answered with horny jaws and horny teeth. The inductive impulse for grasping organs leads not to the balancers typical of the newt host, but to suckers characteristic of the frog.

Whatever goes on in the reacting target tissue in response to an inducer obviously goes on within the limits of that tissue's species-specific capabilities. Cells can develop autonomously only those structures already programmed in their genetic material. The skin cells are thus not faced with a choice between balancers and suckers, or between horny mouth parts and true bony teeth—if they are newt cells they can respond only by making balancers and bony teeth. Experimental manipulation thus cannot swamp out the autonomous expression of the inherited individuality of the cell. If, for example, the embryonic limb bud of a crested newt is covered over with transplanted palmate newt ectoderm, a chimeric leg with typical palmate newt skin develops. The skin retains its own inherited species characteristics even through metamorphosis, never taking on properties of the host, though it usually is lost later as a result of an incompatibility reaction (p. 87). Autonomous, inherited, cell individuality is also responsible, in humans and other warm-blooded animals, for the failure of skin and organ grafts from extraneous donors to "take". The grafts are attacked by the host until they are rejected or resorbed. Getting around this problem is perhaps the greatest challenge facing modern surgery.

Double-headed Beings and Other Monsters

Now and then a calf with two heads and six legs will be exhibited at a county or state fair, usually among the sideshows. Monsters of many kinds are known to occur in all sorts of animals and in humans as well. Among laymen, such malformations tend to be regarded as grotesque curiosities or, where human birth defects are involved, as something frightening and tragic. For the scientist, however, such cases of abnormal development represent "experiments of nature"—he wants to learn what has "gone wrong", hoping thereby to gain a better understanding of the fundamental processes underlying all of development, as well as knowledge of more direct applicability to the medical problems of congenital malformations.

Now that we have become familiar, to some extent at least, with the mechanism of action of the embryonic inducers, we can attempt to explain several characteristic malformations. In doing so, we will be relying on experimental findings to bolster our arguments. We can constrict a newt embryo at the early gastrula stage in such a way that the hair loop divides the organization center into two symmetrical halves (Fig. 28a). The material of the archenteron roof is thereby forced to move inward and then forward in two separate streams. Each half is thus provided with head inducer. The later-involuting region possessing rump-tail inducing capability is not divided by the constriction loop, so that tissue integrity is maintained at the posterior end of the archenteron. Each of the two diverging parts of the head inducer will induce a complete, normal, brain primordium in the overlying ectoderm (b). Towards the rear these primordia merge into a single, unified neural plate of the spinal cord region. Subsequent regulative development leads to a viable being called a *Duplicitas anterior* (anterior duplication), with two well-formed front parts connected to a common rear section (c). Several years ago, in Russia, a human

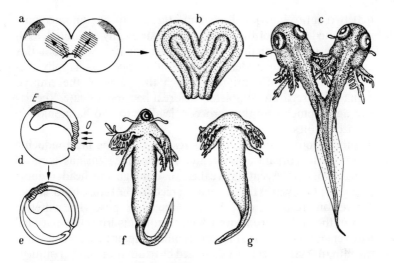

Fig. 28a—g. Malformations in Amphibia. a Symmetrical constriction of an early newt gastrula; "organizer" region hatched diagonally, with arrows showing the direction of invagination of the head-inducing material; head ectoderm dotted. b Anterior duplication in the neurula stage and c in the larval stage. d Damage (arrows) to the head-inducing region of the organizer (*O*, hatched) at the beginning of gastrulation. e Impaired inductive interaction of organizer (hatched) with ectoderm (*E*, dotted) leads to cyclopia (f) or to anencephaly (g) in which the anterior part of the head is missing. (c after H. Spemann, f after H. B. Adelmann)

child (or should we say pair of children?) was born with basically the same body organization as the newt duplication shown in Fig. 28c. The two heads showed a considerable degree of individuality: it sometimes happened that one cried while the other slept peacefully. This *Duplicitas* died of an infection at the age of 13 months.

It is not hard to imagine that an embryo can also be operated upon in such a way that the head inducer remains intact while the posterior part of the archenteron roof becomes split. This leads to a posterior duplication *(Duplicitas posterior)*, i.e. to an animal with four hind legs and two tails. Naturally the depth of the cleft, whether anterior or posterior, can vary considerably. It can happen that only the outermost parts of the heads, or only the tails, are duplicated. Or the splitting can be so drastic that two entire individuals remain attached to one another only in a limited region of the trunk. Unless surgically separated, such "Siamese twins" remain joined together for life. Seen from this angle, normal human identical twins now appear as happily successful cases of duplication in which the parts of the embryo managed to separate completely before it became too late. Regulative development can thus proceed, leading to two harmoniously formed wholes.

Another group of malformations results when the head-inducing region of the organization center is defective. Various sorts of experimental intervention weaken or damage the head inducer (Fig. 28 d). One way is to cut out a big piece of the future head-inducing region from the dorsal lip of the blastopore. The anterior part of the archénteron roof which then forms from the marginal leftovers is much reduced in size. Similar impairments result when the same dorsal lip region is damaged by irradiation or by treatment with certain chemicals. The affected region either does not invaginate normally, so that the anterior part of the "organizer" does not become properly established, or it does come to underlie the brain region of the neural ectoderm as usual, but remains deficient in its effectiveness as head inducer (Fig. 28 e). The brain primordia which form above such defective inducer regions are diminished in size. All degrees of smallheadedness (microcephaly) up to and including the total absence of the anterior part of the head (anencephaly, Fig. 28 g) have been observed. Quite frequently the forebrain remains underdeveloped, with not enough diencephalon material for two eye cups of normal size. The eyeballs which develop are thus smaller than normal (micropthalmy), and it is not unusual to find them extremely close together or even partly fused (synopthalmy). If the shortage of diencephalon material is even more severe, a single cyclopean eye forms in the middle of the forehead (Figs. 28 f, 25 e). The Cyclops myths of the ancient Greeks were probably suggested by actual observations of single-eyed malformations.

Now of course not all head malformations can be explained as defects in the inducing system. The reaction system can also fail occasionally, whereby the ectoderm is not competent to respond fully to the normal inductive stimulus. And finally, normally induced full-sized embryonic brains and eyes can later become

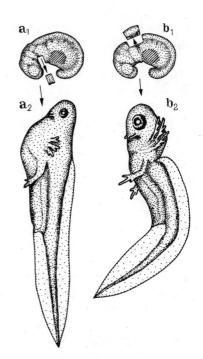

Fig. 29a and b. Influence of nutrient supply on eye growth in the alpine newt. a Removal of the heart primordium. b Control animal with a dorsal defect. (After E. Hadorn and P. Walder)

stunted. An experimental finding to this point occurs when the heart rudiment is removed from an advanced newt embryo (Fig. 29a). This intervention hinders the later blood supply to the eyes and anterior part of the head. The delivery of nutrients from the yolk-rich endoderm (diagonal hatching) is thereby interrupted. The previously normally developing eyes are particularly sensitive to this lack; they stop growing and then they begin to degenerate. Thus, despite normal inducer function, a typical microphthalmy results (a2). If on the other hand chunks of tissue are removed at the same stage from the back region (b1), the nutrient supply is unaffected and eyes reach normal size (b2). The surgery, which has severed the spinal cord, does result in another sort of deformity, however: the lower part of the back is bent under *(kyphosis)*. Thus far we have been dealing with examples of naturally occurring malformations which can be mimicked by deliberate experimental intervention. We have seen that different outside influences can lead to identical or very similar malformations. What are the factors responsible for the naturally occurring birth defects? Where do they act? To what extent are the naturally occurring and experimentally produced defects comparable?

We do know that in all living things abnormal development can be due to abnormalities in the chromosomes and genes. Thousands of genes are involved in normal development, and every so often one or another of these is changed or lost. In the great majority of cases such mutations are fatal. Carriers of these hereditary defects (lethal factors) very frequently die during development because vital processes and organs are missing or function improperly. Other damaged individuals survive, but as deformed or enfeebled creatures. A mutation affecting the head inducer would lead to essentially the same malformations of eyes and brain observed in experimentally damaged embryos (Fig. 28). Moreover, examples are known of genetic factors which act only after the primary induction phase (cf. Fig. 29), leading to growth impairment and ultimately degeneration in the eye primordium. In several species of cave fish the embryonic eyes disappear more or less completely. Here the genetically determined blindness is tolerated without any danger to the animal's viability. A local blockage of the blood supply affects merely the eye region.

Malformations provoke feelings of wonderment; they provide mysterious motifs for fantasy and fable. It is all too easy to forget that what is really fantastic is not the abnormal but the normal—the harmonious development before our eyes of an intricate organism from a single cell. The course of normal development is so unbelievably demanding that the astonishing thing is that development succeeds as often as it does. Certainly, external influences and gene mutations can lead to malformation, but, all in all, the normal development of living things is extraordinarily well safeguarded against innumerable possible disasters.

Chimeras, Parabiosis and Sexual Development

The classical chimera of Greek mythology is a monster with the head of a lion, the body of a goat and the tail of a dragon. Centaurs, sphinxes, minotaurs and sirens are among the other fabulous beings which are not to be found in the natural scientist's book of animals. So it is perhaps all the more astonishing that true chimeric beings can be "produced" nowadays in the laboratory. For this, amphibian embryos are particularly suitable.

We can take one late gastrula each from the alpine newt and the palmate newt and cut them into equal-sized front and rear halves. Then we exchange front halves and press them on to

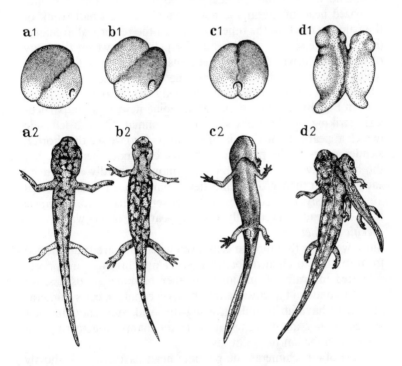

Fig. 30a—d. Chimeras and parabiosis. a 1—d 1 Four different interspecific combinations, shown shortly after operation; the large half is always from the alpine newt, the smaller is always from the palmate newt. a2 Foreparts alpine newt, hindparts palmate newt. b2 Foreparts palmate newt, hindparts alpine newt. c1 Operation for producing side-by-side chimera. c2 Side-by-side chimera from below; right side of body—alpine newt, left side—palmate newt. d1 Healing together in parabiosis. d2 Parabiotic pair: left—alpine newt, right—palmate newt. (After E. Hadorn and H. Rutz)

the rear halves from the other species. The alpine newt embryo is somewhat larger and more darkly pigmented than the palmate newt gastrula (Fig. 30a1 and b1). In no more than half an hour the pieces have become permanently healed into a new whole. Provided the operation has been dexterously performed, these interspecies chimeras mature into viable larvae, which are frequently capable of successful metamorphosis to the land form. A fine example of a pair of successful chimeras is shown in Fig. 30a2 and b2. On the left (a2) we see the bulky foreparts and oversized head of the alpine newt seated on the small trunk of the palmate newt. In the other partner to the reciprocal exchange (b2, right) we see the small head of a palmate newt on the body of an alpine newt. The color patterns make it easy to identify which species the different parts of the body belong to.

Chimeras along the length of the body can also be produced (c1). In Fig. 30c2 the long, powerful alpine newt legs are particularly striking on the right side of the animal. On the left side (which appears on the right in this ventral view) we see the shorter, slenderer legs of the palmate newt. We conclude, therefore, that the body halves joined in chimeric union are hardly affected by each other in their growth and development. Each half develops autonomously, i. e. according to the genetic constitution intrinsic to its cells, leading eventually to the appearance of its own *species-specific characteristics.*

Since we know that foreign cells, even when they are transplanted from mother to child or between sister and brother, are poorly tolerated in grafts of human and other mammalian tissues, we have to wonder a bit why in amphibians even interspecies chimeras appear to have no trouble growing up. And, sure enough, their success is not all it seems at first: the happy togetherness of early development does not last.

In most of our chimeras the palmate newt part gets sick shortly after metamorphosis. Fine blood vessels burst, paralysis sets in, and finally tissues begin to disintegrate and the chimera as a whole is thus doomed to die. What leads to this fatal transformation? At the time of metamorphosis to the land form, glands in the alpine newt skin become active in producing species-specific substances that apparently have a lethal effect on the palmate newt parts of the chimera. These poisons and probably other specific substances are spread everywhere by the common circulatory system.

A further experiment, which we would like to introduce at this point, offers a particularly clear approach to the study of the *incompatibility crisis* (Fig. 30d1). This time we operate at the advanced tail bud stage. From each of the partners which are to be joined a small piece of flank ectoderm is cut away. Then the two embryos are pressed together so that the wounded areas are in contact. The two individuals rapidly grow together into a lasting union. From now on they will lead a common life; they are united in "parabiosis". At first, substances can diffuse from one to the other, and later on the blood of one also circulates in the body of the other. Thus it is possible that both animals can grow normally, even if only one of the mouths is fed and nutrients are taken up through only one intestine. Our Fig. 30d2 shows a parabiotic pair: on the left the larger alpine newt, on the right the smaller palmate newt. Here, once again, species-specific development has proceeded autonomously. The palmate newt has remained small even though it has been just as richly nourished by the common bloodstream as the larger-growing alpine newt partner.

Parabiotic combinations are well-suited to the investigation of a variety of questions. In non-harmonizing parabiotic combinations the course of the incompatibility crisis caused by blood-borne substances can be followed from beginning to end. As in front-to-back and side-by-side chimeras, the palmate newt of our parabiotic pair becomes fatally ill shortly after metamorphosis, dragging his partner down with him to an unfortunate end.

Parabiosis experiments have been particularly informative in studies of *sexual development*. What happens if a male embryo is united with a female one? First we must mention that because the primordia of the distinctive organs have not yet been established, the sex of an embryo cannot be determined at the stage at which the operation is performed. Although the later sex is already foreordained in the chromosomes of the cell nucleus, the sex-determining chromosomes in amphibians are not recognizable by their size or shape. Under the microscope they are indistinguishable from the rest of the chromosomes (or autosomes, cf. Fig. 34). But even if the experimenter is forced to work blind, in about 50 % of the cases he will be combining a genetic female with a genetic male. When both of the partners belong to the same species, the animal genetically predestined to become a female is usually completely masculinized. The embryonic gonad, which would have developed into an ovary in the absence of experimental intervention, now develops into a testis, and a sperm duct develops in place of an oviduct. This transformation is brought about by substances released by the developing testis of the male partner. At first these sex hormones diffuse across the connecting embryonic tissue; later they are spread about by the common bloodstream. A transformation in the opposite direction can also be achieved, provided the female embryo belongs to a larger and faster-growing amphibian species than the male. Now the female sex substances dominate, forcing the gonad to develop into an ovary instead of the testis it would have formed otherwise.

Experiments like these on amphibians help us to understand a long-known experiment of nature. Farmers know from centuries of experience with twin births in cattle that a cow calf born alongside a bull calf is never normal. According to the laws of chance, we would have expected a brother-sister pair in 50 % of all fraternal twin births. But here, too, as in amphibian parabiosis, the genetically female individual becomes masculinized. In cattle the transformation process gets stuck about halfway through, however, resulting in a creature, called an "intersex" or "freemartin", which is neither all male nor all female.

Intersexes are comprised of a mosaic of organs, some of which are nearly completely female and others of which are almost fully male—they show considerable variability in this, with overlapping transitions across the whole range between the two sexes. Intersexes are always sterile and thus can never be used for breeding.

This transformation affecting cattle twins becomes comprehensible when we consider the conditions under which they develop in the womb (Fig. 31). Both embryos establish contact through their respective placentas with the uterine wall of the mother. The suction cup-shaped protuberances, called cotyledons, which form on the placenta fit into corresponding depressions in the wall of the uterus. These connections are the sites of gas exchange and uptake of nutrients. As Fig. 31 shows, the highly vascularized

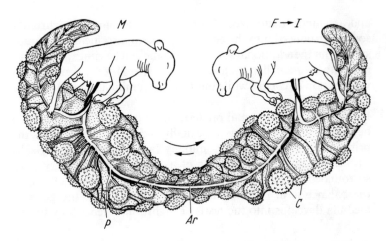

Fig. 31. Natural parabiosis in twin calves. *M* male with visible scrotum. *F* female develops into intersex (*I*). *P* placenta, *C* cotyledons; *Ar* artery (light) connects the two circulatory systems, veins are shown dark. (After F. R. Lillie)

placentas of the twins grow together, leading to a fusion of their blood vessels. We see that a large artery (*Ar*) has established a common blood connection between the depicted twins.

This placental link-up enables the blood of each fetus to circulate in the body of the other, so that hormones produced in one are able to influence the organ development of the other. Most probably the male sex substances are stronger and earlier-acting than the female ones, and thus they affect the sexual development of the cow calf, transforming it to an intersex. It is a lucky thing that nothing similar happens during human pregnancies. A twin sister can develop completely normally alongside her brother, even in those occasional cases when connections can be demonstrated between the embryonic circulatory systems. Why the human fetus, but not the calf, is protected against hormonal disturbances during twin pregnancies remains a puzzle.

Now let us try to understand what is actually involved in bringing about a *sexual transformation* during development. The sex of an organism is initially decided at the time of fertilization by the genes in the chromosomes. In the human, for example, the mature oocyte contains 22 ordinary chromosomes (autosomes) and an intermediate-sized X- or sex chromosome. The chromosomes introduced into the egg by the sperm also include 22 autosomes, but the additional sex chromosome can be either an X-chromosome or a smaller Y-chromosome. The 44 + XX combination will develop into a girl while the 44 + XY combination will become a boy.

Despite this chromosomal predestination every vertebrate animal begins its development as a sexually indifferent being, with the primordia for the two sexes initially being formed side-by-side. The embryonic gonad consists of a central, or medullary part, surrounded by an outer, or cortical part (Fig. 32, middle). Where the balance is in favor of male-determining genes, the gonadal medulla develops into the testis (T, right); in a genetically female

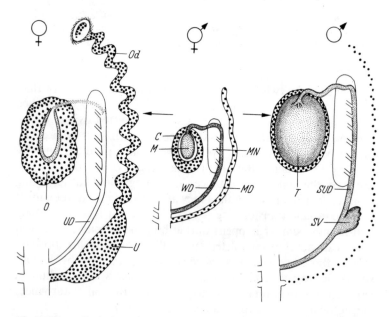

Fig. 32. Bisexuality in the embryonic primordium of the amphibian sexual apparatus (middle), showing *M* medulla, *C* cortex, *WD* Wolffian duct, *MD* Müllerian duct, *MN* mesonephros. *Left*: development into female with *O* ovary, *Od* oviduct, *U* uterus, *UD* urine duct. *Right*: development into male with *T* testis, *SUD* sperm and urine duct, *SV* seminal vesicle. Female rudiments and organs indicated by large dots, male by fine dots

animal, on the other hand, the ovary (O) is constructed from the gonadal cortex (left). The genital ducts, i. e. the exit passages for the germ cells, have been prepared for both possibilities. The male "Wolffian duct" (WD) and the female "Müllerian duct" (MD) run parallel to one another at the early indifferent stage (middle). As soon as either the cortex or medulla gains the upper hand as a result of differential gene action, hormone-like substances are released by the developing ovary or testis which then affect the genital ducts. The medulla promotes development of the Wolffian duct that will become the sperm duct or vas deferens. In Amphibia this duct must also function in conveying urine from the primitive kidney (first pronephros and after metamorphosis mesonephros) so that this duct has both excretory and reproductive functions in the male. The gonadal cortex, on the other hand, stimulates the Müllerian duct to develop into the oviduct (Od) and uterus (U). The flourishing of the male organs is accompanied by the demise of the female primordia. In the male, the cortex gradually diminishes in size leaving a meager remnant, while only traces of the Müllerian duct still remain. In the female the gonadal medulla disappears, as well as the embryonic connection between gonad and mesonephros. The Wolffian duct cannot be sacrificed in female amphibians, however, since it remains indispensable as the urine duct (UD). In mammals, the embryonic mesonephros is only of passing significance as an excretory organ before a new kidney (metanephros) with its own ureter has been established. Hence, the Wolffian duct can be completely dispensed with in females. In male mammals the Wolffian duct remains intact, as in male amphibians, but functions only in transporting sperm from the epididymis which has developed as a derivative of the embryonic mesonephros.

In view of the bisexuality in structure and reactivity of the genital organ rudiments, it is not surprising that the chromosomal sex can be modified or shifted to a greater or lesser extent by a variety of internal and external influences. The sex transformations in parabiosis are accomplished upon this initially "ambiguous" background. On the basis of numerous observations and a large amount of experimental experience we are led to conclude that the differences between male and female cannot be based on any absolute "all-or-none decision". Sex is always something "more or less", whereby the two "normal sexes" can be linked through all gradations of intermediate intersexual levels. The degree of degeneration of the primordia of the opposite sex may vary greatly from individual to individual.

The Male Toad as Mother

Examining a sexually mature male toad (*Bufo bufo*, Fig. 33a) we find, lying close by the testis, an apparently functionless tissue mass, which has been called Bidder's organ (*B*). Nearby, and readily apparent, is the embryonic oviduct (*Od*), still intact. If the testes of this animal are now surgically removed, an impressive sexual transformation results from the castration (Fig. 33b). Bidder's organ develops promptly into a functional ovary (*O*), and during the same time there is a great swelling of the oviduct. A previously male animal, even one which has already fathered

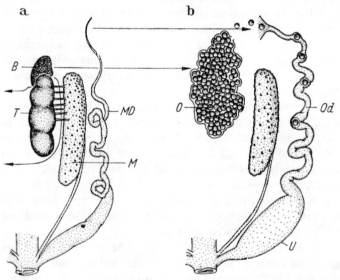

Fig. 33a and b. a Sexual apparatus of a male toad. The testis (*T*) is surgically removed (arrows toward left); *B* Bidder's organ, *MD* remnant of Müllerian duct, *M* mesonephros. b Result of the operation: Bidder's organ has developed into a functional ovary (*O*), the oviduct (*Od*) and uterus (*U*) have grown considerably

children, thereby becomes capable of assuming a female role. This is possible because, along with the development of the female reproductive structures, the hormonal milieu also changes, switching the mating instincts into the female pattern. Such a "*neo-female*" can be mated with a normal male and out of this unusual union of two genetically male animals, normal offspring can emerge and grow to maturity.

The transformation brought about by castration is readily understood in light of our earlier discussion (Fig. 32): Bidder's organ is really nothing else but the not quite completely degenerated cortex of the embryonic gonad. Once the testes have been removed their dominant inhibitory action ceases and, thereafter, the cortical remnant of the embryonic gonad is able to develop into an ovary. Moreover, since the embryonic precursor of the functional oviduct has also been preserved, a complete sex reversal is possible, even in older, fully mature, male toads.

During the early stages of amphibian development, transformation of the chromosomally intended sex can be achieved by a wide variety of means. We have already become familiar with the sex transformation of the female which results when male and female animals are joined in parabiosis (p. 87). To get the same result, it is enough to implant the testis primordium from a male embryo into a genetically female embryo—in this case, also, the recipient will develop into a neo-male. Finally, large numbers of transformed animals can be obtained simply by raising embryos and young larvae of Amphibia in water to which sex hormones have been added.

Neo-males and neo-females can both be used, as in the example we have just seen of the castrated toad, to bring about "same-sex" crosses. The offspring of such "homosexual" matings are what interest us now. What sex will they be if both parents are genetically female? If both are genetically male? Before trying to understand these questions we must explain some of the *basic principles of sex determination.*

Most animals produce approximately equal numbers of male and female offspring. The sex chromosomes insure that this 1 : 1 ratio is maintained, usually by one of two basic mechanisms. In flies, grasshoppers and most bugs, as well as in mammals, each female has two X-chromosomes in addition to the autosomes, while each

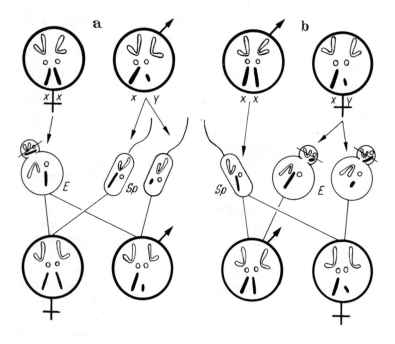

Fig. 34a and b. Diagram of sex determination for the cases of female (a) and male (b) homogamy. ♀ female; ♂ male. Two pairs of autosomes are shown in each case (white). A sex chromosome (black) can be either a long rod-shaped X-chromosome or a short Y-chromosome. *Top row:* the diploid parent generation. *Middle row:* the haploid germ cells at the conclusion of the maturation divisions; *E* eggs with polar body (only one is shown and it is crossed out to indicate that its chromosomes take no further part in what happens; see also Fig. 4, p. 12), *Sp* sperm. *Bottom row:* the new diploid generation formed at fertilization

male has one X-chromosome and one Y-chromosome (Fig. 34a). As a result, maturation of the gametes in the female leads to only one kind of egg (E), each containing one X-chromosome, whereas males produce two kinds of sperm (Sp) with equal frequency, those with a female-determining X-chromosome and those with a Y-chromosome which are male-determining.

The females in such cases are therefore designated as the "homogametic", and the males as the "heterogametic", sex. In the case of butterflies, moths and birds the sex is determined by an analogous mechanism, but with the chromosomal roles reversed. Now it is the male who is homogametic; he provides only one kind of sperm, all with an X-chromosome, while two kinds of eggs ripen in the heterogametic female: ones with an X-chromosome alongside ones with a Y-chromosome. In addition, we should mention those animals (certain bugs and moths) which regulate their sex determination without a Y-chromosome. The homogametic sex has, as usual, two X-chromosomes, while the heterogametic sex contains, besides the autosomes, only a single X-chromosome. In order to find out which sex is the homogametic one, and which the heterogametic, two classical methods are available. One method is direct and uses the microscope. The chromosomes of dividing cells are investigated according to number, shape and size. In favorable cases, such as that shown in Fig. 34, one is able to distinguish the sex chromosomes directly by their individual characteristics, and to recognize both XX and XY pairs. The alternative procedure is indirect. It depends on the fact that the X-chromosome, like all other chromosomes, contains hereditary factors. In humans, genes affecting red-green color vision and blood clotting, among others, are located on the X-chromosome. If these normal genes mutate, color blindness or hemophilia results. And from the inheritance of such "sex-linked characteristics" it is then easy to perceive which sex has two X-chromosomes and which only one. Unfortunately, both methods fail to work for amphibians. Although one can determine the chromosome number of salamanders, frogs and toads quite exactly, and even distinguish individual chromosomes by their size and shape (Fig. 5), no one (as we have already said, p. 87) has succeeded in identifying the sex chromosomes. Amphibians are, moreover, not suitable animals for convenient genetic experimentation; in fact, no one has yet been able to demonstrate an hereditary factor bound to the sex chromosome of any amphibian.

In this difficulty we are helped by the fact that matings are possible between animals of the same genetic sex. At this point we want to describe an experiment which was successfully carried out by R.R. Humphrey, an American. He worked with the axolotl (*Ambystoma mexicanum*), a type of salamander (see Fig. 10) which becomes sexually mature as a larva, and which we will encounter again (p. 127). The course of the entire experiment is diagrammed

95

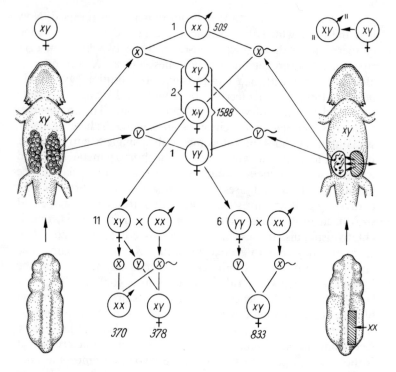

Fig. 35. Demonstration of female heterogamy in the axolotl. Eggs shown as small circles, sperm as small circles with tail; ♀ female, ♂ male, "♂" neo-male. Further explanation in the text. (Adapted from R. R. Humphrey)

in Fig. 35. First the presumptive gonad region is removed from one side of an embryo and replaced by the corresponding region from another individual (diagonal hatching, lower right). Because the sex of the animals cannot be determined at the time of the operation, the experimenter is once again working "blind". Still, in about a quarter of the cases he will produce the combination which interests us: a genetic female into which an embryonic testis has been introduced. The strong hormonal influence emanating from such a male implant is able to switch the development of the host's gonad, which now becomes a testis instead of the ovary originally prescribed by the host's chromosomes (upper right). By cutting open the abdomen of each host animal several months after the initial operation, it is possible to identify those in which a transformation from ovary to testis is taking place. As soon as the transformation is complete, the implanted testis (diagonal hatching) is surgically removed from the other side of the animal.

The result of this first phase of the experiment is a neo-male, with a single functional (sperm-producing) testis, which can now be mated with a normal female (left). If the female sex in axolotls— as in humans—is the homogametic one, then in a mating of neo-male × female both parents would be XX animals and only females could emerge from such a "same sex" cross (XX × XX). Instead, from seven matings of neo-males with normal females, Humphrey recovered 509 males (24.3 %) and 1,588 females (75.7 %), thereby closely approximating a Mendelian 1 : 3 relationship. This result is immediately understandable if we assume that the female is heterogametic. Then, gametes with an X-chromosome or a Y-chromosome would occur in both female and neo-male with equal frequency.

The diagram shows the possible combinations (1 : 2 : 1) for the cross XY × XY. The resulting males (25 %) are genetically identical (all belonging to the XX-class) while among the females (75 %) two genotypes, which are not directly distinguishable, must occur. Along with the 50 % which are normal XY-animals there should be another 25 % which are YY individuals. The latter would be novel laboratory creations not occurring in nature.

Further crosses proved this interpretation correct. Seventeen females from among the 1,588 in the daughter generation were allowed to grow to maturity and then paired with normal (XX) males. Of these, eleven produced a progeny (left) which was evenly divided statistically between males (370) and females (378). Obviously, the mothers must have been XY females. On the other hand, the remaining six mother axolotls (right) had 833 daughters and not a single son. An exclusively female (XY) progeny like that is just what we would expect when XX is crossed with YY. And not only could the XY and YY females be thus distinguished from one another; the validity of the whole interpretation was nicely confirmed by the fact that there were about twice as many XYs as YYs among the randomly chosen seventeen animals.

97

Thus, by a laborious yet exciting and ingenious route, it was proved that in the axolotl it is the female sex which is heterogametic (XY) and the male which is homogametic (XX). Similar same-sex crosses have also been realized in other amphibian species: we have already seen how a castrated male toad can become a mother (p. 92, Fig. 33). The union of several of these neo-females with normal males gave rise to an exclusively male progeny of 1080, and therefore, in toads as in axolotls, the males are homogametic. Interestingly, male-male matings of axolotls and female-female matings of toads led to the same conclusion.

The simple chemical expedient of adding female sex hormone to the culture water will transform male larvae of the South African clawed toad *(Xenopus)* or of the Spanish newt *(Pleurodeles)* into neo-females. Once again the union of two genetic males leads to a purely male progeny; thirteen *Xenopus* crosses produced 940 offspring, all male, and from six *Pleurodeles* crosses, 1,624 males were obtained. Therefore in these species, as well, we represent a cross between two genetic males as XX × XX. There are also amphibians, however, for which there is convincing experimental evidence that the female is homogametic; a case in point is the European grass frog *(Rana temporaria)*. So we see that each species and group among the Amphibia presents its own special problems to the researcher interested in the clarification of sex inheritance. Finally, we should note that zoologists often reserve the designation X and Y for cases where the male is heterogametic. For those animals with heterogametic females they have chosen to use the letters W and Z for the sex chromosomes. The formula used for humans and for frogs would thus be given as "female (XX) × male (XY)", while for toads and axolotls one would have to write "female (WZ) × male (ZZ)". For our purposes we have not bothered with this really unnecessary distinction.

On the Migration of the Primordial Germ Cells

Rather surprisingly, we find in many vertebrates and invertebrates that the primordial germ cells, from which eggs and sperm are later derived by division and differentiation, are initially not located in the mesodermal gonad primordium. In many vertebrates they are first visible within the endoderm. This means that the primordial germ cells often must migrate great distances from their extragonadal place of origin in order to reach the region where the embryo is constructing its testes or ovaries. The functional gonad, then, consists of two parts: a *"gonadal soma"*, formed from the somatic cells of the individual, and the *germ line cells*, destined to form the gametes which will initiate the following generation. The gonadal soma resembles a flower bed, the soil of which nourishes the growing plants: the blood vessels of the gonadal soma furnish nutrients to the germ cells, while other parts form seminiferous tubules or become the follicle cells in which the egg is embedded. In vertebrates, moreover, the cells of the gonadal soma deliver hormones necessary for sexual maturation and reproduction.

First of all we want to follow the migration of the primordial germ cells, using the frog embryo as an example. We are helped in this by a very welcome marker characteristic. At the vegetal pole of the uncleaved egg there are several highly stainable cytoplasmic inclusions. These polar granules are then incorporated during cleavage into individual cells (Fig. 36a). All the cells that receive polar granules—and only these—become primordial germ cells. Polar granules are known to contain a large amount of ribonucleic acid (RNA), and it is possible that these specific RNA molecules could contain the information for the special germ line developmental program. In any case, the endoderm cells which surround the primordial cells but which receive no polar granules have a completely different developmental fate: they become cells of the gut tube.

If the vegetal pole of an unfertilized frog egg is irradiated with ultraviolet light the polar granules are damaged and subsequent formation of the primordial germ cells is drastically reduced or even prevented altogether. This radiation damage can be specifically corrected by the injection of unirradiated cytoplasm from the vegetal pole region. During the cleavage period the primordial germ cells marked with polar granules migrate upward between the cells of the endoderm, finally reaching the floor of the blastocoel (Fig. 36b). When the upper edges of the endoderm fold over after gastrulation to form the gut tube (p. 49) the primordial germ cells are located like "foreign bodies" in the roof of the

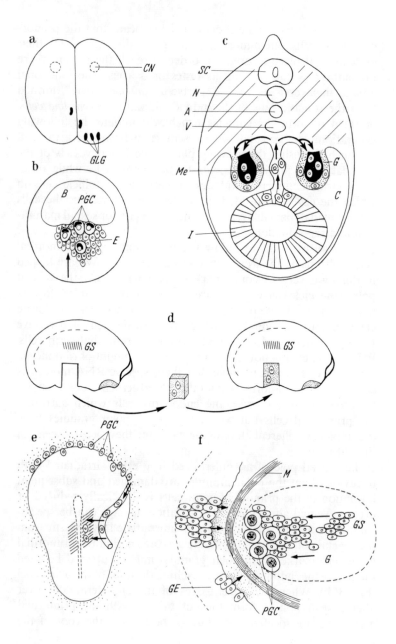

100

gut. This is the place at which the gut becomes attached by a tissue bridge, the dorsal mesentery, to the wall of the body cavity. The migration route of the primordial germ cells continues up this dorsal mesentery (Fig. 36c). As our figure shows (arrows), having once reached the top the primordial germ cells distribute themselves to both sides of the body, eventually coming to populate the medulla and cortex of the gonad primordium. As was mentioned on p. 90 (Fig. 32), the vertebrate gonad is initially bisexual. If the medulla develops further, a testis is formed; if the cortex continues to grow, an ovary results. Primordial germ cells which have migrated into the medulla become sperm while those in the cortex become eggs.

The foregoing description is based on direct microscopic observations during embryonic development. At appropriate times the primordial germ cells, which are usually bigger than the somatic cells and morphologically distinguishable from them, can be seen at various places along their supposed route of migration. The accuracy of these observations can be tested by transplanting a piece of tissue containing primordial germ cells from an animal carrying a stable "genetic marker" differing from that of the host. In one such experiment a piece of endoderm containing primordial germ cells is removed from a late neurula of the clawed frog *Xenopus* and then transplanted, as shown in Fig. 36d, into another

◄ Fig. 36a—f. Migration of the primordial germ cells (*PGC*) into the gonadal soma (*GS*). a Position of the germ line granules (*GLG*) in the two-cell stage of the common European frog *(Rana temporaria)*, *CN* cell nucleus. b Same embryo as in a at the blastula stage; *B* blastocoel (cleavage cavity). Germ line granules seen as cell inclusions in the primordial germ cells as these cells migrate upward within the endoderm (*E*). c Diagram of the migration route into the gonadal primordia (*G*). Medulla black, cortex dotted, *I* intestine, *C* coelom, *Me* mesentery, *V* vein, *A* aorta, *N* notochord, *SC* spinal cord. d Transplantation of a piece of endoderm containing primordial germ cells between clawed frog *(Xenopus)* embryos. The gonadal soma (*GS*) into which the cells eventually migrate is shown hatched. e Chick embryo, with primordial germ cells at the front edge of the embryonic shield. Blood vessel transports primordial germ cells to the gonadal soma (hatching), where they leave the circulatory system. f Attracting substances emanating from the still germ cell-free germinal epithelium (*GE*) of a chick embryo pass through a membrane *M* and bring about directed movements of primordial germ cells (large nuclei) in an already populated gonad (*G*): the affected cells attempt to leave the gonadal soma (small cells, *GS*). (a and b after L. Bounoure, d after A. W. Blackler, f after R. Dubois)

embryo, where it heals into place. As donor and host, one can use two clawed frog subspecies in which the ripe eggs have a characteristically different size and color, or one can use the number of nucleoli as a marker, by taking wild type animals with two nucleoli per cell and heterozygotes for the *onu* mutant (Fig. 9) having only one nucleolus in each cell.

Now if our description of the origin and migration of the primordial germ cells is correct, the sexually mature host animal carrying such a transplant should produce gametes with donor-specific marker characteristics. And, indeed, a female whose own eggs would have been large and dark-colored actually does produce small, light-colored eggs typical of the other subspecies which furnished the implant. And where an *onu* heterozygote has been used as donor, a host animal whose somatic cells have the usual two nuclei begets offspring with a single nucleolus. The presence of the "genetic marker" in the progeny proves that their hereditary material is derived from the donor.

Transplantation experiments of the type shown in Fig. 36d incidentally provide us with a further important insight. The transplanted primordial germ cells are derived from embryos whose nuclei contain either two male-determining X-chromosomes or the female-determining XY combination (p. 98). What happens when XX-primordial germ cells populate the gonad soma of an XY-host? In this situation the cortex of the gonad primordium develops into an ovary, without regard to the immigrated germ cells, and the germ cells simply adapt to this. Although they have been genetically programmed to become males they develop instead into normal eggs which give rise to offspring. In *Xenopus* the sex is thus determined by the *chromosomal genes of somatic cells of the gonad* and not by the germ cells.

After having become familiar with the migratory history of the primordial germ cells in anurans (frog-like Amphibia), it is perhaps a bit of a surprise to learn that in urodeles (tailed Amphibia) these cells are at no time located in the endoderm. They are already found near the gonad primordia early in embryonic development, when they become segregated from the lateral plate mesoderm. From there they do migrate, but over a rather short distance, upwards and into the gonadal primordia. In humans and in other mammals the primordial germ cells are again initially found in the endoderm, as in the frog. In mammals, in fact, they are even located outside the body of the embryo, namely at the base of the umbilical cord.

As we did earlier for other migratory cell types, we can now ask how the primordial germ cells stay on the proper path and what causes them to come to rest at a specific location. A particularly fine start towards answering these questions is possible in experiments with chick embryos. Here the large primordial germ cells are located initially in the endoderm around the front edge of the blastodisc or embryonic shield. The gonadal soma develops far away, in the central mesoderm of the middle germ layer. If the primordial germ cells of the embryo are destroyed by local irradiation or if the region in which they are located is excised, a sterile chicken develops, one with testes or ovary but without sperm or eggs. In normal development the primordial germ cells leave their starting location as soon as the blood vessels of the yolk sac circulation have developed. They invade the blood vessels and are then propelled along by the blood stream. Although they presumably travel through various regions of the body, they all "get off at the same stop"—the gonadal soma. Here and only here do they leave the bloodstream, working their way through the vessel wall to settle down in the gonad primordium (Fig. 36e).

This behavior can be analyzed more closely. A gonad already populated with germ cells is isolated and cultivated as an explant in tissue culture. Next to this gonad is placed a piece of still unpopulated gonadal soma (germinal epithelium), and then a membrane is interposed between the two explants. The yolk sac membrane, which encloses the yolk of the chicken egg, is suitable for this. In this experiment the primordial germ cells which had been uniformly distributed in the young gonad now migrate towards the piece of germinal epithelium. Because of the way in which this particular experiment has been designed, they cannot actually settle in the empty gonadal soma—the membrane prevents this. But other experiments have shown that, if given the chance, these emigrants will settle in the unpopulated gonadal tissue. The cells of the germinal epithelium evidently give off substances which can diffuse through a membrane and mobilize settled primordial germ cells to "pick up and leave". In normal development the attracting substance would have to penetrate the walls of the blood vessels, give the "get off at this stop" message to the primordial germ cells as they travel past, and get them to leave the bloodstream in the direction of the gonadal soma. If this is actually what does happen, and several of the details are still only hypothetical, it is an example of *positive chemotaxis*. In any case the chick experiments show that migrating cells change their behavior as a result of specific chemical influences and move in a directed way.

Color Pattern and Color Change

The Amphibia are beautifully colored animals. European newts have bright yellow bellies, and at mating time the male alpine newt additionally displays a shining blue-silver streak along his side. We marvel at the pure green of the tree frog, and at the fascinating array of yellow, reddish, green, bluish and black hues of many frogs of the genus *Rana*. Some of these colors are due to specific pigment substance, such as the melanins (brown to black) or the pterines (yellow to red). Riboflavin also contributes to the yellow color of the amphibian skin. Other color effects, especially the various degrees of blue, depend on the structure of the skin layers. These are the "physical colors" or "structural colors" which appear when light is shone on thin stacked plates or turbid media. The green color that is so common among amphibians, reptiles and birds is due to the combination of pigment yellow and structural blue.

Melanins and other pigments are usually contained in particular cells called pigment cells or *chromatophores*. We can distinguish the dark melanophores, the yellow xanthophores and the red erythrophores. Finally, there are also cells which shine bright silver because they reflect the light totally. If such iridocytes (or iridophores) also contain yellow pigment, they produce a lovely golden sheen.

Chromatophores are star-shaped cells. In amphibians most of them lie spread out just beneath the transparent epidermis, but some are also found in deeper skin layers. Pigment cells also give the iris of the eye its color and they line the inner surfaces of the body cavity wall (peritoneum).

occur in a motley mixture. One pigment may be evenly dispersed in one type of cell, while a second pigment is clumped together in another. Through independent variations and shifts of the different pigments, numerous colors and shadings can be achieved. The location of pigments in the chromatophores is controlled by specific substances, some of which are released by the hypophysis, or pituitary. We encountered this hormone-producing gland once before (p. 4). Among other functions, it brings about sexual maturation and release of the germ cells. With respect to its developmental origin, structure and function the hypophysis is a complicated organ indeed. Its posterior lobe develops from the floor of the diencephalon (Fig. 38a). Attached to this "nervous part" there is a "glandular part", the anterior lobe, which is derived from an outpocketing of the ectodermal mouth cavity. Where the anterior and posterior lobes border on one another there is, in many vertebrates, including the Amphibia, yet another distinct zone, the *pars intermedia*. The cell area that has been determined to make the anterior lobe and *pars intermedia* is still located on the embryo surface at the tail bud stage. These primordia can therefore be excised quite easily (Fig. 38b). Embryos without the glandular part of the hypophysis develop remarkably well; they grow up into something closely approaching normal larvae. Yet they are immediately recognizable by virtue of their lighter color. In all the chromatophores except for those at the tip of the tail, the pigment is present as an extremely condensed dot (Fig. 38c). This is due to the fact that the hypophysectomized animals lack a hormone which normally causes the pigment to spread out. More detailed investigations showed that in the normal animal this dispersing hormone comes from the *pars intermedia*, hence the name *intermedin* sometimes given this substance. It is now more commonly referred to as *MSH* (melanocyte stimulating hormone).

The action of the hypophysis in affecting color is also easy to demonstrate in the adult frog. If a pituitary extract is injected its skin darkens considerably within a short time. Other hormones work in the opposite direction. *Adrenalin* from the adrenal gland turns the frog unnaturally pale because it promotes pigment clumping. Lately it has been proved that an outpocketing on top of the diencephalon, long designated by the anatomists as the *epi-*

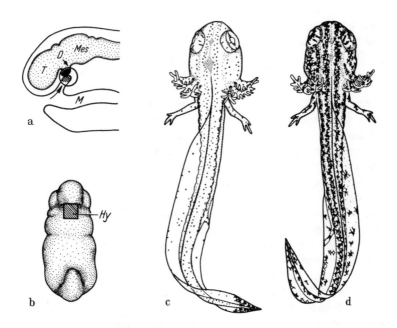

Fig. 38a—d. Hypophysis and color change. a The embryonic primordium of the hypophysis is circled: the anterior and middle lobes (hatched) are derived from Rathke's pouch (arrow) in the roof of the mouth cavity (*M*). Posterior lobe (black) comes from the floor of the diencephalon (*D*). *T* telencephalon, *Mes* mesencephalon. b Amphibian embryo seen from below shows in the hatched area the still superficially located material of the future anterior and middle lobes of the hypophysis (*Hy*). This piece is excised. c Newt larva which developed from hypophysectomized embryo (b): the pigment within the pigment cells is, with the exception of the tip of the tail, clumped together, giving a light appearance. d Normal control larva of the same age as c—the pigment is spread out within each pigment cell. (c and d after experiments of M. Gandolla)

physis or pineal organ (and once suspected to be the "seat of the soul", since it had no other obvious function), also releases a hormone which influences color change. This so-called *melatonin* functions like adrenalin as an antagonist of MSH, producing a lightening of the body color. Melatonin also influences certain rhythmically occurring metabolic processes.

Pigment shifts are not only controlled by hormones via the bloodstream; in many animals they are under the direct control of special color change nerves. But since nerve endings also give off hormone-like substances, it is hardly a fundamental difference for the reacting target organ (in this case a pigment cell) whether the regulation is "neural" or "hormonal". As a rule the reactions under nervous control are more rapid than those dependent upon hormonal influences. It is tempting to pursue the question of how the color change is effected by hormonal or nerve-mediated stimuli. But since this book is concerned with developmental processes, we shall have to turn instead to a series of experiments which contribute to our understanding of the origin of the pigment cells.

In newt larvae the first pigment cells become visible shortly after the embryo has stretched out into a motile young larva. In many newt species they appear principally in two long rows (Fig. 40c), giving one the impression that they must be derived from the local epidermal cells. But appearances are deceiving. With the exception of the pigment cells of the eye the entire arsenal of colored cells on the surface of the body is derived from a single embryonic location, the *neural crest*.

We saw earlier that the central nervous system is first laid out on the surface as a plate surrounded by thick folds (Fig. 17, p. 51). After the plate has closed over in the midline the crest material lies above the dorsal seam of the neural tube. But these cells of the neural crest cannot keep still. Obeying a remarkable dispersal drive, they migrate out in various directions (Fig. 17c2). And in so doing they show an ability bordering on the miraculous to find their specific places. Once they have reached their ultimate destinations these ectoderm cells differentiate into all kinds of different organs and tissues.

Some of the neural crest cells travel throughout the body just beneath the epidermis and it is these that are the future pigment cells of the skin (*P* in Figs. 17c2 and 39). At the time of their migrations they contain no pigment; the pigment is not synthesized in the cytoplasm until the cells have reached their final locations. Other derivatives of the neural crest are depicted in Fig. 39. We will merely list them at this point. Some fill the interior of the protruding larval fin (*FM*), others assemble themselves alongside the neural tube and form the spinal ganglia, one pair per segment (*SG*, also in Fig. 17c2). In these ganglia are to be

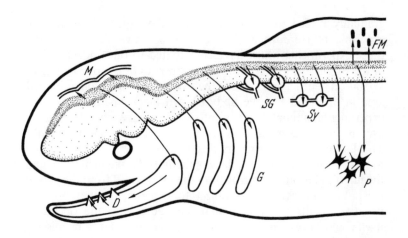

Fig. 39. Neural crest derivatives include the following cell types and parts of organs: *P* pigment cells, *SG* spinal ganglia, *Sy* sympathetic ganglia, *FM* fin mesenchyme, *G* gill arches and jaws, *D* dentine core of the teeth, *M* meninges of brain

found the cell bodies of the sensory nerves, their fibers making contact with the spinal cord on the one hand and connecting up with the peripheral organs on the other. Other clusters of cells unite to form the ganglia of the sympathetic nervous system of the visceral organs. Particularly remarkable is the fact that the same source which produces pigment and nerve cells is also able to provide cells for cartilaginous parts of the skeleton. The gill arches and jaws (*G*), as well as parts of the base of the skull are formed from strings of cells that move downward from the neural crest. In the jaws themselves these much-travelled cells form the dentine core, i.e. the bone-like material of the teeth (*D*). Still other cells of the neural crest envelop the brain, developing into the different meninges (*M*) of the brain. Finally, other neural crest cell populations contribute to the formation of the adrenal medulla.

It is astonishing to discover that developmental programs of such impressive versatility are to be found within the little heap of embryonic neural crest cells. Knowledge of the almost inexhaustible inventory of developmental achievements of these cells was gradually pieced together from a large number of remarkable experiments. Here we shall have to be selective, describing only those experiments which have contributed to our understanding of the origin and pattern-forming properties of the pigment cells. We take a neurula and remove the two neural folds from a limited area in the middle of the body (shown black in Fig. 40a). This experimental animal develops into a robust larva (b) which, however, is missing pigment cells in a band of skin around its middle. The larval fin is missing in this region as well. This appears to prove that in normal development both pigmentation and the impulse for outward growth of the fin proceed from the neural crest. Yet one can always object to experiments that produce negative results by arguing that damage due to the operation itself could be responsible when something turns out to be missing or something doesn't go right. Experiments which show directly that pigment cells are derived from the neural crest, and only from it, are therefore considered better proof. One can start by transplanting a piece of the neural crest onto the mid-belly surface of a host embryo. An island of color will develop around the implant in the otherwise pigmentless region. Or we can make an ectoderm sandwich of the type shown in Fig. 24 and fill it with a piece of neural crest material. The explant soon becomes generously populated with pigment cells. But how do we know that the pigmented cells are derived from the neural crest implant? How do we know that the implant does not merely induce pigmentation in nearby host cells? Here again, by using appropriate cell markers (p. 45) it is possible to demonstrate conclusively that the pigment cells are of neural crest origin.

Particularly impressive results have been obtained from transplant experiments in which a piece of neural crest from one species is replaced by the corresponding piece from another species. The two Californian newt species *Taricha torosa* and *Taricha rivularis* are particularly suitable for such "*heteroplastic transplantations*". In *torosa* the melanophores arrange themselves in two compact stripes running the length of the animal (Fig. 40c), while a pattern of rather uniformly scattered cells is characteristic for *rivularis* (d). As the result of an exchange transplantation experiment we see that the implant has produced a zone with the typical *rivularis* pattern on the *torosa* larva (e), and that the *rivularis* larva has

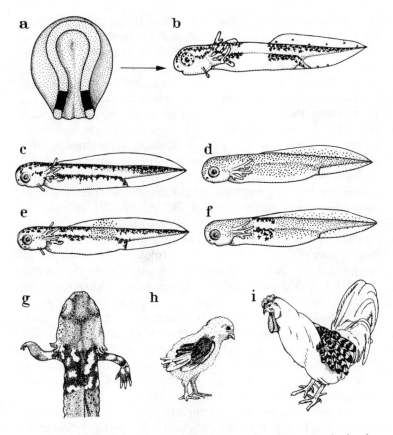

Fig. 40a—i. The neural crest as origin of pigment cells. a Newt neurula showing the regions (black) where its neural crests were removed. b Alpine newt which has developed from neurula a. c *Taricha torosa.* d *Taricha rivularis.* e *T. torosa* with *rivularis* implant. f *T. rivularis* with *torosa* implant. g Older *torosa* larva with axolotl implant. h Chick of the White Leghorn strain with American robin pigmentation (dark) in the wing feathers. i White Leghorn rooster at an age of 2 1/2 years with feather pigmentation due to pigment cells derived from the peritoneum of a Barred Rock embryo. (c—g after experiments of V. C. Twitty and D. Bodenstein; h and i after M. E. Rawles)

a belt of pigment of the *torosa* type (f). These experiments provide us with several important insights. First of all, we note that the loose community of *torosa* cells migrates over long distances through foreign territory and still is able to assemble into bold stripes of cells not typical for the *rivularis* host. The migrating cells have thus retained not only their determination to form pigment cells, but their *species-specific pattern-forming qualities*, as well. It is not at all obvious that this should be so. Apparently the *torosa* cells mutually attract one another while in the same environment the *rivularis* cells tend to avoid one another. Such positive and negative affinities (p. 55) must therefore be genetically determined cell properties able to function autonomously in a foreign host. Genetically established qualities of pattern formation can also be demonstrated in combinations of less closely related species. In Fig. 40g we see a newt larva of the species *Taricha torosa* just before metamorphosis. Behind its gills, and also to some extent on its forelegs, it has areas of splotched skin quite atypical for this species. The cells forming this pattern are derived from a piece of the neural crest of an axolotl (*Ambystoma punctatum*) which was introduced into the newt embryo at the neurula stage. Here, too, the host does not influence the hereditary pattern-forming capabilities of the migrating cells. On the other hand, there is evidence from several experiments with heteroplastic combinations that the pigment cell distribution can also be influenced by the host. As an example, we can see in the larva of Fig. 40e that the *rivularis* cells come to a stop at the level of the lower *torosa* stripe. Yet in *Taricha rivularis* itself they continue to migrate ventrally beyond this point (d).

Interactions of this sort between migrating cells and their surroundings are involved in bringing about all color patterns. Somehow the future pigment cells have to "notice" when they have reached the goal of their journey; how else would they be able to find their ways so reproducibly to their place of rest! In this, they behave rather like the migrating primordial germ cells (Fig. 36). We have seen that the tendency of certain isolated propigment cells to strive to get away from one another (Fig. 19) can serve to explain the uniformly scattered pigment pattern of the *rivularis* type (Fig. 40d).

Up to now we have limited ourselves almost entirely to experiments with amphibians. From the results of a great number of other experiments we know that the cells responsible for body pigmentation in all vertebrate animals are derived from the neural crest.

This has been beautifully demonstrated for birds and mammals. In Fig. 40h we are presented with a member of a white strain of chickens which during an early embryonic stage had received implants of future pigment cells from the neural crest of the brown-pigmented American robin (*Turdus migratorius*). Where the pigment cells of the implant have come to rest the feathers have the dark pigmentation of the robin donor. Note however that the feathers themselves are not derived from the implant; they are proper chicken feathers. The incorporated pigment-forming cells from the robin have simply come to rest at the base of the feather germ. They stay at this site of feather outgrowth throughout the life of the animal. These "settler" melanophores with their delicate cell extensions surround the feather forming cells and supply them with pigment granules. Similar processes occur at the roots of the hair in mammals. Constant melanin production and delivery ensure that the hair remains colored. Only with advancing age do the chromatophores situated at the root of the hair lose their ability to form new pigment. The hair that grows out thereafter is pigmentless, but appears white due to the reflection of light by the network of cells which comprise the hair.

To conclude our discussion of pigment patterns we would like to present a showpiece experiment (Fig. 40i). A wing primordium is cut out of a three day old chicken embryo of the White Leghorn strain. At this early stage the cells of the neural crest have not yet settled in the future wing area. The excised wing bud is now implanted in the body cavity (coelom) of an embryo of the Barred Rock strain. As the implant develops, future pigment cells from the peritoneum migrate into the implant and provide the feather germ with pigment granules. It is really remarkable that the pigment cells of peritoneum, which normally have nothing to do with feather color, are able to take over this unusual task. After the host has hatched, a small darkly pigmented wing can be removed from its body cavity. This implant can be transplanted once more, on to the back of a one day old White Leghorn chick. The second host now develops into a handsome chicken of the kind shown in Fig. 40i. Wing feathers having the typical color banding of the Barred Rock strain grow out from the implant. The feathers themselves, however, are constructed by the original

White Leghorn cells of the embryonic implant. The pigment cells alone were taken from the opposite strain (first host). There is nothing about the implant to indicate that its pigment cells are from the belly region. They behave at the growth zone of the White Leghorn feathers just like the skin pigment cells which normally migrate in directly from the neural crest. These pigment cells remain active for years and at molting time continue autonomously to provide new feathers with pigment patterns characteristic of their own strain of origin.

On Wound Healing and Regeneration

Let's start right off with an experiment. A rectangular piece of epidermis is cut out of an older newt larva (Fig. 41a). After the amazingly short time of 24 hours the gap is closed over and the wound is healed. A closer examination reveals what processes are involved. First there is a heavy accumulation of cells at the edge of the wound; coming from all sides they slide over the breach, covering it completely. These cells have moved in directed fashion from the surrounding epidermis to the edges of the wound. This *cell migration* proceeds even after the wound is closed. The result is a much greater than normal density of cells in the wound region. These goings-on can be more precisely grasped by counting, some 3—4 days after the operation, the number of epidermal cells per unit area in the various zones, i.e. in the wound area itself, in its nearby environment, and in skin farther away from the wound. It turns out not to be necessary to take into account all the cells, but only the large, conspicuous, light-colored gland cells, since they migrate into the wound area to the same extent that their less conspicuous brethren do. Cell counts on the side that was operated on can be compared to those from the other, undisturbed, side. In Fig. 41a we have indicated the cell number by the density of the dots. Calling the normal density 100%, we can find, in the wound region, accumulations up to 150% (densely dotted). This build-up implies a corresponding cell loss in regions immediately surrounding the wound. And in fact we find cell densities in these border regions that are reduced by 50% in comparison to the normal case (sparsely

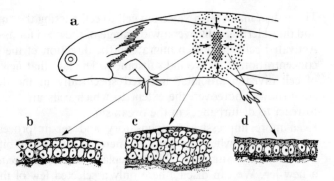

Fig. 41a—d. Cell migration in wound healing. A rectangular wound is made in a newt larva (a). Cells migrate in from the surrounding areas (short arrows) and cover the gap (dense dotting). b Piece of epidermis from outside the zone of influence. c Accumulation of cells in the wound region. d Section through the depletion zone. (After E. Hadorn and P. S. Chen)

dotted). This depletion area extends around the wound for quite appreciable distances. Outside this zone the normal cell density is maintained (intermediate dotting). The differences in the cell numbers can be seen very clearly in microscope sections. In the normal skin (b) we usually find two layers of gland cells. In the wound zone the thickened epidermis can have as many as four such layers (c), while in the depletion zone (d) only single gland cells in a single loosely packed layer are to be found.

These observations make it clear that wound closure in the epidermis is not due to a local increase in cell division, but rather to cell immigration from regions bordering on the wound. Only after completion of these cell migrations, that is, only after a week or so, do compensatory processes set in, including a phase of cell division in the depletion zone.

This picture of wound healing is not valid only for newt larvae, but is characteristic of wound healing in the epidermis in general. Wounds in the integument of insects are closed in much the same way. A number of interesting questions come up: what mobilizes the remote epidermal cells? What shows them the way to the edge of the wound? Probably special stimulants, sometimes called "wound hormones", are formed at the site of the wound.

115

These then make their way from cell to cell passing the "message" and thus alerting cells over a wide range of the need for assistance. Activated cells must then migrate in the direction of the greatest concentration of the wound substances. The fact that new rounds of cell division are later initiated specifically in the depletion zone shows, moreover, the extent to which cells are "finetuned" to react to disturbances in the organism.

Even more impressive compensatory and repair processes are set in motion when the leg of a newt is cut off or bitten off. The mutilated animal is able to replace the loss; it *regenerates* a new leg. We can discuss here only a selected few of the many findings which have resulted from careful study of the processes of regeneration. Let us look first at what actually happens when

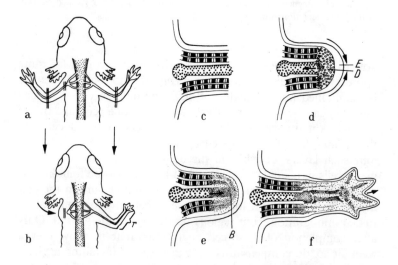

Fig. 42a—f. Leg regeneration in tailed amphibians. a The double lines show the site of amputation; on the left side the nerve connection to the leg is also severed. b Right: regeneration (*r* is the regenerated piece) left: resorption of the stump (arrow). c—f Sequence of events following amputation. c White: epidermis, cross-striated: muscle, dotted: cartilage or bone. d The epidermis (*E*) grows over the wound; underneath the tissues disintegrate (*D*) forming dedifferentiated cells (circles). e Blastema formation (*B*, tiny dots) succeeds dedifferentiation, marking the beginning of regeneration. f Outgrowth of the regenerate (tiny dots) to form a complete leg; skeletal structure becoming visible

a newt or salamander leg is regenerated. The foreleg can, for example, be amputated just above the elbow (Fig. 42a and c). One day later, the wound is already covered with skin (d). Here, too, this occurs by overgrowth of the open region by epidermis cells. Damaged cells and cell debris in the interior at the wound region are then taken care of, i.e. eaten up, by white blood cells, the macrophages. Next, a remarkable process begins beneath the surface of the epidermal closure. At the point of the cut, cartilage, bone, muscle and connective tissues of the upper leg stump disaggregate into single cells. This disintegration proceeds up the arm (arrow in d) but comes to a stop once an appreciable quantity of cells has been set free. At the same time that the cells dissociate from the former tissue masses they lose their functional structure. They become "de-differentiated". Former cartilage, bone, muscle and connective tissue cells take on the form of undifferentiated cells, no longer readily distinguishable from one another. The result of this retrograde development is a *regeneration blastema* (*B* in e) composed predominantly of like-appearing cells. This collection of cells subsequently behaves just like an embryonic leg bud. It grows in size by cell division and begins to sprout forth, thus gradually replacing the missing piece (f). At the same time new cartilage, bones, joints, tendons and muscles are laid down and then differentiate within the regenerate. In this way the newt regains a normal foreleg.

Let us stop to think for a moment what a remarkable accomplishment this regeneration really is. It is extremely important to note that "old", already differentiated, cells are capable of being transformed back to a state which permits them to proliferate rapidly, and which enables the proliferated cells to take part in renewed, secondary, developmental processes.

With this we have come up against a very controversial subject. Are the new skeleton and the new muscle formed from "dedifferentiated" cells that have retained their original tissue-specificity or can a former muscle cell now also develop into cartilage and bone? The term *metaplasia* is used to describe a process of the latter sort whereby a differentiated cell (or a cell derived from it) is able to become transformed into a differentiated cell of another type. In the present case this developmental plasticity would involve dedifferentiation to a multipotent state, similar to those often found in primary embryonic blastemas, followed by redifferentiation in a new direction. Lately those contending that metaplasia is involved in limb regeneration appear to have been losing ground. What is lacking are incontrovertible experimental results which would show that the blastema cells really can enter upon totally new paths of differentiation. Still, there is one classical experiment which cannot be ignored. If the upper arm bone left in the stump after amputation of the foreleg is surgically removed, the lower arm and hand will nonetheless regenerate with all the skeletal elements formed completely normally. Skeletal regeneration is thus possible even when the skeletal elements of the stump can take no part in the formation of the blastema. It is thought that connective tissue cells that have retained the developmental potency to make bone may help out in this case. That metaplasia really does occur in at least one regenerative process will be shown when we discuss lens regeneration later in this chapter (p. 120).

The events occurring in regeneration blastemas are comparable with the regulative processes in embryonic cell systems. The available material is disposed of according to a fixed plan so that from arbitrarily sliced and randomly recombined component parts a unified whole can emerge. Thus half a leg blastema can regenerate an entire extremity while two whole blastemas, after being fused together, will form only a single leg.

We may therefore assume that the embryonic construction plans do not disappear after completion of their initial tasks, but rather are still available in the adult organism. The "extremity field" which guides embryonic leg development is retained in the completed leg as a latent organizational capacity.

It is remarkable that in the course of regeneration the phase of tissue disintegration comes to a halt after a certain time and that the succeeding growth and differentiation in the blastema begin at the proper time. There are sound reasons for assuming that the growing barrel-shaped blastema exerts an inhibitory effect on the tissues higher up the arm, halting further disintegration. The nervous system is involved in this expedient regulatory scheme. If, as shown in Fig. 42a, the arm nerve coming from the spinal cord is severed on the left side in addition to the forearm amputation, the tissue disintegration beginning at the wound surface and moving up the arm simply fails to stop. The whole leg stump is affected. The tissue debris are unable to unite to form a blastema in the absence of the normal nerve connection, instead they disintegrate totally and are resorbed. And so the amputated leg gradually disappears before our eyes (Fig. 42b).

A similar thing happens after X-ray treatment. If both forelegs of a newt or salamander are damaged with equal radiation doses and if then on one side the lower arm or hand is cut away, the remaining stump undergoes complete destruction, while the uncut leg remains intact in spite of the irradiation. Apparently the experimenter, by cutting off the outermost part, sets into motion the first phase of regeneration, the tissue disintegration, which then, however, proceeds unchecked because the correcting antagonistic effect of blastema formation fails to occur. A successful regeneration thus depends on the finely tuned interplay between destructive and constructive processes.

The *function of the nerves* is probably to deliver *material assistance*. The substances provided are synthesized in the cell bodies of the ganglion cells which are located either in the spinal cord (motor) or in the spinal ganglia (sensory) (Fig. 39). Nerve fibers originating in these cell bodies lead to the periphery, in this case into the regeneration blastema. It is known that substances are constantly being transported outward along these fibers. Whatever it is that the nerves bring to the regeneration blastema, it is evidently quite indispensable. Astonishingly, however, the embryonic limb buds require no nerve connection in order to develop. They grow outward and differentiate into normal legs even when any and all nervous connections have been experimentally severed. Evidently the embryonic primary blastemas have requirements and potencies different in some respects from those of the secondarily formed regeneration blastemas.

The extremities of the tailed amphibians are preferred objects of regeneration research because newts and salamanders can still replace their tails and legs after metamorphosis. Even new eyes will regenerate from leftover parts of the old organ. It has also been possible to remove an eye from a salamander and replace it with another one. After a certain installation and remodeling period the animal is able to see with its implanted eye. By contrast, the capacity for regeneration in frog-like amphibians appears to be severely restricted. Though tadpoles are able to regenerate tail and limbs, after metamorphosis a frog no longer can replace a leg that has been cut off. It has been shown that the scar tissue which forms under the skin as it rapidly heals over hinders formation of a proper blastema. If one prevents the over-hasty wound closure by treating the stump with a strong salt solution, leg regeneration can be initiated in a frog, as well. Success can also be attained when the nerve supply is augmented by routing additional nerves into the leg stump. These surprising findings have taught us that the potential for regenerative achievements is much more widespread than was previously thought. But, to get success, experimental intervention to create special circumstances is required.

Regeneration experiments on newts have provided a rich variety of additional findings. Among these is a particularly famous and classical regeneration experiment reported in 1891 by the Italian V. S. Colucci. More than any other, it stimulated the best minds of the day, and not just biologists, but a number of philosophers as well. Colucci showed that a newt eye from which the lens had been removed would regenerate a new lens from the material at the border of the dorsal iris (Fig. 43a—d). Several years later this ability was reinvestigated by G. Wolff and exhaustively evaluated on a theoretical basis. What makes the so-called *Wolffian lens regeneration* so unusual is that during embryonic development the lens is formed from the epidermis and never from the iris (Fig. 25). After it has hardened into cornea, the tissue of origin is no longer capable of regeneration in this case, yet completely different tissue is able to take over the replacement function. To the vitalists who wanted to attribute special, non-physical, non-chemical, forces to the living organism, this lens regeneration appeared to provide a convincing example of goal-directedness in living things. Indeed, the eye does know how to take care of itself, and this has to impress us just as strongly today as it impressed the discoverers of lens regeneration more than half a century ago. Now, however, we have insights from newer experiments which show us that experimental analysis of cause and effect can clarify much that at first seems mysterious.

The dorsal margin of the iris evidently retains throughout life a latent capability to form lens. But why is this competence only

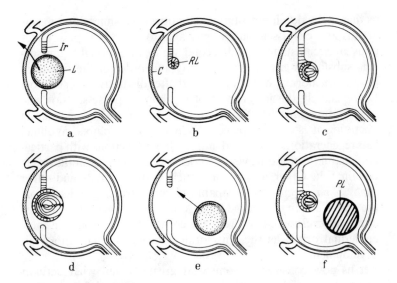

Fig. 43 a—f. Lens regeneration from the dorsal margin of the iris (*Ir*). a Removal of lens (*L*, arrow); lens is originally derived from the corneal epidermis (*C*, shown finely dotted). b—d The dorsal iris margin (hatched) forms a new lens (*RL*, regenerating lens). e Displaced lens inhibits regeneration (arrow). f "Dead" lens encased in paraffin (*PL*) fails to inhibit lens regeneration

realized when the legitimate lens is removed? It is possible to show that the initial lens exerts an inhibitory effect on the iris, keeping the lens-forming tendency of the iris cells in check. This effect is still present when the lens is removed from its normal position and implanted in the vitreous humor of the rear eye chamber (Fig. 43e). If however a lens is impregnated with paraffin before reimplantation is loses its control over the iris margin and regeneration promptly begins. The inhibition is thus not due merely to the presence of a spherical body or to the mechanical pressure exerted by it. The lens acts instead through chemical agents produced by its living cells, and only when these specific lens substances are lacking does the latent capability of the iris margin become freely active.

The peculiar case of Wolffian lens regeneration is thereby placed within a framework of wider significance. First of all, it shows us that many developmental potentialities lie a-slumbering in our organs and cell assemblages, only able to come into play under unusual circumstances. And, second, we see that special organ-specific substances ensure the harmony and order of the organism both in the normal healthy state and after disruptive intervention. Unfortunately the iris margin of the human possesses no lens-regenerating capacity. When the lens is removed in a cataract operation it is never replaced. Even in the Amphibia, Wolffian lens regeneration is not found universally. It functions with particular reliability in the newts (*Triturus* species) and, in addition, in certain fish. Other amphibians, such as the axolotl and other *Ambystoma* species are incapable of reconstructing a lens from the dorsal iris. In the clawed frog *(Xenopus)* the regenerate formed after lens excision comes from the cornea, that is, from the same epidermal origin as the lens formed during normal embryonic development.

Let us now consider in somewhat greater detail what actually has to happen in order that a lens can be formed from an iris. The differentiated cells of the iris, which are stuffed full of pigment granules, begin to dedifferentiate as soon as they receive the chemical "message" that the eye no longer has a lens. First they lose their pigment, then they begin to divide once again and form a lens blastema, which differentiates into a lens. This is then *true metaplasia*, which is to say that a specific cell group switches from one program of genetic expression to another. Genes which were active in pigment synthesis cease to function. Previously quiescent genes now become active, making possible the synthesis of specific lens proteins.

Hormones and Metamorphosis

Countless tadpoles populate our fresh waters during springtime. In summer these larvae then transform themselves in just two weeks into lung-breathing animals. Someone strolling along the edge of a lake or pond may encounter thousands of little young frogs as they all leave the water together and hop up onto the dry land. This change to a new environment is preceded by a metamorphosis, one that involves drastic transformations in many parts of the body and in numerous organ systems.

122

As first sign of these changes in the tadpole ripe for metamorphosis, the hindleg stumps begin to grow out rapidly and the forelegs, which had lain hidden in the gill cavity during the tadpole stage (Fig. 45), break through the overlying skin and become free. The tail is resorbed until it completely disappears. Multicellular slime and poison glands develop in the skin as its structure is otherwise becoming adapted for life on land. The gills disappear; the frog now uses his lung sacs and mouth cavity for absorption of oxygen from the atmosphere. The whole larval mouth armament with horny jaws and horny teeth is discarded, the mouth becomes widened into a frog's mouth and true teeth emerge from the jaws. A tongue is also formed in the mouth. The eyes grow to a respectable size and are equipped with lids, while a tympanum (ear drum) is formed to close off the middle ear from the outside. In the interior there are reconstructions and alterations in the circulatory system and musculature. The function of the larval pronephros is taken over by the mesonephros. The vegetarian tadpole has an intestine nine times its body length; during metamorphosis the length of the gut is reduced to twice the body length and is converted to the needs of the carnivorous (fly-eating) frog.

There are also biochemical changes accompanying the various regressions, alterations and new constructions within the organ systems. At metamorphosis the oxygen carrying ability of the blood is reduced in keeping with the conversion to air breathing. This adaptation is accomplished by the construction of two different hemoglobins, one before metamorphosis which has a higher affinity for oxygen and one after metamorphosis with lower affinity. This means that there is a succession in the expression of different genes carrying coded information for the protein part of the hemoglobin. "Tadpole genes" are replaced in their activity by "frog genes". Each of the different genes codes for a different protein chain (p. 27). The frog red blood cells can, moreover, be distinguished microscopically from their larval counterparts and even the organs which produce red blood cells are different in the two developmental stages: in the larva it is the kidney, in the metamorphosed frog the spleen.

A comparable conversion in blood formation has also been demonstrated for humans. Before birth the continuous resupply of red blood cells comes from the liver, while afterward the bone marrow takes over this task. The iron-containing pigment (heme) of the prenatal "fetal hemoglobin" is nestled in globin protein consisting of two identical α-globin chains and two γ-chains. The α-gene remains active in the production of the postnatal "adult hemoglobin". In contrast, the γ-gene is shut down and its function is assumed by a newly activated β-gene. Therefore, in place of the γ-chains two β-chains are formed after birth. Different sequences of base "code words" in the DNA are responsible for the differences between β- and γ-chains. Different sequences of amino acids are consequently built into the two hemoglobin proteins (p. 27). This conversion in the synthesis of hemoglobin molecules shows us once more that, in the development of an organism, genes come into action stepwise, replacing one another in a definite order in time and space.

A further molecular change occurs during frog metamorphosis in the synthesis, starting with vitamin A, of the light-absorbing pigment of the eye. The pigment *visual purple* (porphyropsin), suitable for underwater vision, is replaced by a molecule (rhodopsin) adapted for life on land. Finally we can mention the change in the chemistry of excretion. Tadpoles swimming in the water are able to dilute sufficiently the poisonous ammonia resulting from protein catabolism and excrete it directly. Land animals, with less water available, have to find a way within the body to render the poisonous ammonia harmless. Typically this is taken care of by using the ammonia to synthesize urea or uric acid. Thus, just as we do, the "land frog" eliminates urea in its urine. To accomplish these changes in excretory metabolism, new enzymes not present in larvae are required.

In the tailed amphibians, also, metamorphosis leads to a long list of changes. Though the tail is retained in newts and salamanders, the alterations in the skin, circulation and respiratory apparatus are not less profound than those in the tailless amphibians.

Amphibian metamorphosis confronts the researcher with a number of interesting problems. We will see shortly that pursuit of these questions led to discoveries of significance far beyond the world of the amphibians.

Let us first ask about the mechanism by which metamorphosis is triggered. In the year 1912 F. Gudernatsch reported an experimental success which has gone down as one of the pioneer achievements in the history of biology. Young tadpoles were fed pieces from various sheep organs: lungs, heart, gut, musculature, brain and various glands. It was found that those animals which had eaten powdered thyroid gland reacted immediately by initiating premature metamorphosis. No such effect was obtained with material from any of the other organs. Four years later a further crucial experiment succeeded. The embryonic thyroid gland primordium, which develops in the floor of the pharynx, was cut out of a number of frog embryos. These animals developed unimpeded into vigorously active larvae. While their brothers and sisters among the control animals that had not been operated on, but otherwise had been raised under identical conditions, began to transform themselves at the appropriate time into frogs, the thyroidectomized animals remained ever true to life in the water. They did not metamorphose, but grew instead into giant larvae. That it was not the "operation in itself" which was responsible for the failure can be demonstrated either by feeding the thyroidectomized animal thyroid substance or by implanting a thyroid gland from another animal anywhere in the body. In both cases metamorphosis is promptly triggered.

Uncounted later experiments confirmed these fundamental discoveries: without a *thyroid gland* there is no metamorphosis, and premature transformation will result if thyroid material is supplied. These insights were obtained more than half a century ago, at the time when the first great discoveries were being made concerning those active substances that we all know today as the *hormones*. The thyroid belongs to the class of glands without an exit duct, the endocrine glands, whose only connection with the rest of the body is through the blood stream. Their active substances are released as "internal secretions" into the blood and are then carried to the target organ. The cells of the thyroid have the specialized property of being able to concentrate iodine from the food and water which enters the body. This element becomes incorporated into relatively simple organic compounds that are synthesized in the thyroid, and it is these substances that are effective as metamorphosis hormones. Nowadays such iodine-containing substances can be prepared in pure form. Among them the compound called *thyroxin* has a particularly powerful effect in triggering metamorphosis. Thyroxin from the chemical shelf can completely take the place of a functional thyroid gland. Unbelievably small amounts of this substance suffice to induce premature metamorphosis in tadpoles. One merely adds the hormone to the water in which the tadpoles are living. If we have a school of young tadpoles in a liter bottle, say, then in order to get metamorphosis we need add only one hundreth of a milligram of thyroxin, which corresponds to a dilution of $1:100,000,000$. The active material from the thyroid contains other hormones besides thyroxin, all chemically related and all containing iodine. We now understand why tadpoles raised in iodine-free water and on iodine-free food never metamorphose.

Microscopic investigation of the thyroid gland shows that its cells remain small and inactive throughout the whole of larval life. Only just before metamorphosis does the production and release of hormone begin. There are tropical amphibians which do not go through a free-living tadpole stage during their development. Thus, fully metamorphosed, but very small, lung-breathing young animals hatch from the egg coats of a certain tree toad which lives in Jamaica. In such species hormone formation in the thyroid also begins very early, shortly after embryonic development.

In light of such experiences we have to ask whether the thyroid gland itself, following its own developmental clock, can determine the time of hormone release and thus the initiation of metamorphosis. The answer is provided by a series of decisive experiments which have been summarized in a table for the sake of clarity. We will see that besides the thyroid the *hypophysis* also plays a role. We have already mentioned (p. 106) that the embryonic primordium of the hypophysis can be removed, and that this will affect the body color of amphibian larvae (Fig. 38). Remarkably, animals lacking the anterior lobe and the *pars intermedia* of the hypophysis grow into large larvae. But these tadpoles (Exp. 2), just like the thyroidectomized ones (Exp. 1) fail to undergo metamorphosis. The various experiments are presented in Table 2. Obviously *both* endocrine glands are indispensable for the completion of the transformation. We have already seen that addition

Table 2. Importance of hypophysis and thyroid gland for metamorphosis

	Hypophysis	Thyroid	Supplement	Metamorphosis
Control	present	present	—	yes
Expt. 1	present	absent	—	no
Expt. 2	absent	present	—	no
Expt. 3	absent	absent	thyroxin	yes
Expt. 4	absent	absent	hypophyseal hormone	no
Expt. 5	absent	present	hypophyseal hormone	yes

of extraneous thyroid hormone can trigger metamorphosis (Exp. 3). A similar direct effect is not found upon addition of hypophyseal hormones (Exp. 4). The mode of action of substances from the hypophysis is indirect— it triggers the subordinate thyroid to make and release thyroid hormone (Exp. 5). Now we know the essential processes. At the proper time the hypophysis releases a hormone aimed at the thyroid gland. This *thyrotropic hormone* stimulates the thyroid and enables it to furnish the rest of the animal with metamorphosis hormone. It is only this latter substance which acts directly on the many target organs, each of which then accomplishes its unique transformation.

There are quite a few amphibians which either normally do not metamorphose or never metamorphose. Among these is the Mexican axolotl *(Ambystoma mexicanum)*, a large salamander species which remains in the larval stage throughout its whole life and which reproduces as a larva, also. Yet if one feeds these overripe larvae pieces of thyroid tissue or gives them thyroxin, they will transform into the land form. Careful investigation of the axolotl case has shown that it is not primarily the thyroid which fails, but its trigger, the hypophysis. The absence of metamorphosis is, of course, an hereditary characteristic, which must have appeared at some time or other by mutations in the genetic material of normal predecessors still capable of metamorphosis. One or more genes which normally control the function of the hypophysis have been changed. In other non-metamorphosing amphibian species from America, mutations have occurred which directly block thyroid function.

127

Another "genetic defect" is present in the European grotto olm (*Proteus anguineus*). This colorless, blind, cave animal lives in the subterranean waters of the Karst Mountains in Yugoslavia. Olms never metamorphose; throughout life they keep their external gill branches, aquatic skin and all other larval properties. Neither thyroid nor hypophyseal hormone brings about metamorphosis in olms. Even a piece of olm skin implanted into a metamorphosing salamander does not go along with the changes occurring in its new environment. In the olm it is the target organs which fail. The responsiveness of the various larval organs to the hormones has been totally lost through mutation.

Differential response to metamorphosis hormones is something we should consider somewhat further. Is it not highly remarkable that in response to thyroxin the tail musculature of a frog larva regresses completely while in the same animal, and hence in the same hormonal milieu, the muscles of the trunk remain quite intact? And in addition, the leg muscles even show a positive reaction—they *grow* intensively in response to hormone. Such astonishing differences have inspired a number of interesting experiments. An eye primordium can be implanted into the tail bud of a frog embryo. What develops is a tadpole carrying around a very nice eye in its tail region (Fig. 44a). When metamorphosis sets in later on, the eye located in the tail remains unmolested (b). To the extent that the tail disappears, the eye gradually moves closer to the end of the body, finally sitting on the frog's hindquarters (c). Similar results are obtained with implanted leg primordia (Fig. 44d). They, too, in no way follow the destructive tendencies of their surroundings but grow instead into good-sized legs (e), which after the disappearance of the tail emerge directly from the trunk of the body (f).

On the other hand, if a tail bud is transplanted into the embryonic trunk region, it first grows out as a powerful tail (g) but then at metamorphosis is resorbed just as quickly as the normal tail (g—i). Successful action of the metamorphosis hormone thus depends not on the location within the body, nor on the immediate surroundings, but on the tissue-specific properties of the organs themselves. Tail muscles which appear to be so similar to trunk muscles apparently have different chemical properties nevertheless, so that one kind is adversely affected by thyroxin and the other

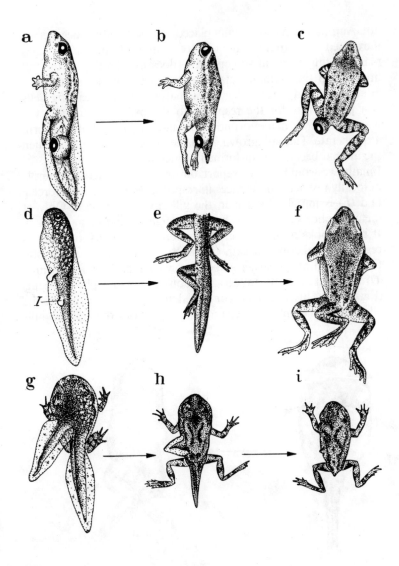

Fig. 44a—i. Different responses to metamorphosis hormone. a—c Eye implant in disappearing tail remains intact. (After J.L. Schwind). d—f Leg bud implant (*I*) develops into a leg growing out of the tail and remains intact. (After M. Schubert). g—i Tail is resorbed even when implanted in the trunk region. (After R. Geigy)

not. Amputated *Xenopus* tails placed in tissue culture degenerate if exposed to thyroxin in the culture medium. In newts and salamanders this thyroxin susceptibility does not develop in the tail muscles, so they remain intact during metamorphosis. In frogs, attainment of a certain degree of maturity in the reacting cells is a prerequisite for the response to thyroxin. If a tadpole tail is cut off before metamorphosis the tadpole first begins to form a regenerate. This still growing tail then does not disappear when the animal becomes transformed at metamorphosis.

Finally we would like to report on another instructive example of locally restricted differences in response. In tadpoles the foreleg bud (*F*) is initially hidden in the gill cavity (Fig. 45a). Only at metamorphosis do the legs break through a window in the skin. It really looks as if the leg, by its contact stimulus, causes this regional breakdown in skin tissue. But if one removes the still tiny leg bud at an earlier stage (arrow in Fig. 45a), an opening (*O*) in the skin forms anyway as soon as metamorphosis begins (Fig. 45b). This might be compared to a hole occurring at the elbow of an empty sleeve, though a possible role of the gills

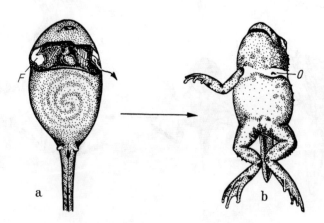

Fig. 45a and b. Foreleg break-through in the frog larva. a Tadpole in which the right foreleg (*F*, light) is still hidden in the gill cavity and the left foreleg has been surgically removed (arrow away from foreleg stump). b Same animal during metamorphosis; the right leg has broken through the skin covering; an opening (*O*) has also formed on the left. (b after H. Braus)

in bringing about the perforation cannot be ruled out. In any case the experiment demonstrates that a narrowly delimited region of the skin system reacts during metamorphosis in a manner different from the rest of the skin.

A number of further experiments have shown, however, that this classical experiment is actually quite difficult to interpret. For one thing, the hole which self-differentiates in the absence of leg influence is significantly smaller than the skin opening on the opposite side where no surgical removal of the leg primordium took place (Fig. 45b). Apparently at least two reinforcing influences are at work: an autonomous tendency to disintegrate in the skin cells themselves and the effects of the outward thrusting leg. The perforation of the skin may thus be an example of a "doubly-assured" or "fail-safe" developmental process.

If this interpretation is correct, skin pieces from the region where the window normally forms ought to perforate during metamorphosis in a foreign location (e.g. on the back) as well. On the other hand, a skin transplant into the forelimb region from any other part of the body would be expected to become perforated by the action of the underlying leg. Such experiments have been carried out; they have unfortunately not produced consistent, unambiguous, results. A conclusive and universally convincing proof for double assurance of a developmental performance has not been forthcoming.

In their totality, the processes of metamorphosis in the Amphibia show us the marvelous interplay between the triggering hormones and the reactions of the various target organs. Our wonderment at such well-ordered achievements of the living system can only increase when we reflect that each of hundreds of genes must intervene at the right time and place to guide this harmonious development to completion.

Suggestions for Further Reading

Balinsky, B. I.: An Introduction to Embryology, 3rd ed. Philadelphia: Saunders 1970.

Davidson, E. H.: Gene Acticity in Early Development. New York: Academic Press 1968.

DeHaan, R. L., Ursprung, H.: Organogenesis. New York: Holt, Rinehart and Winston 1965.

Ebert, J. D., Sussex, I. M.: Interacting Systems in Development, 2nd ed. New York: Holt, Rinehart and Winston 1970.

Gurdon, J. B.: The Control of Gene Expression in Animal Development. Oxford: Clarendon Press 1974.

Kühn, A.: Lectures on Developmental Physiology, 2nd ed. Berlin, Heidelberg, New York: Springer 1971.

Markert, C. L., Ursprung, H.: Developmental Genetics. Englewood Cliffs, N. J.: Prentice-Hall 1971.

Saunders, J. W., Jr.: Animal Morphogenesis. New York: The MacMillan Company 1968.

Trinkaus, J. P.: Cells into Organs: The Forces that Shape the Embryo. Englewood Cliffs, N. J.: Prentice-Hall 1969.

Twitty, Victor Chandler: Of Scientists and Salamanders. San Francisco: W. H. Freeman and Co. 1966.

Waddington, C. H.: Principles of Development and Differentiation. New York: The MacMillan Company 1967.

Watson, J. D.: Molecular Biology of the Gene, 2nd ed. New York: Benjamin 1970.

Willier, B. H., Weiss, P., Hamburger, V.: Analysis of Development. Philadelphia: Saunders 1955.

Index

135

136

Wolff, G. 120
Wolffian duct 6, 63, 90, 91
— lens regeneration 120—122
wound healing 114—118, 120

Xenopus laevis 5, 30—33, 41, 42, 65, 98, 101, 102, 122, 130

Xenopus laevis test 5

yolk 7, 8, 38, 44, 47, 67, 83, 103
— plug 47, 49
— sac 103

zygote nucleus 13, 14, 39, 41

J. Brachet:
Introduction to Molecular Embryology

67 figures. Approx. 180 pages. 1973
(Heidelberg Science Library, Vol. 19)
DM 14,40; US $5.60
ISBN 3-540-90077-2
Distribution rights for U.K., Commonwealth,
and the Traditional British Market (excluding
Canada): English Universities Press Ltd.,
London

Prices are subject to change without notice

This book, written with all the authority of a
leading developmental biologists, offers a
fascinating tour of the puzzles of molecular
embryology. Although written for a non-
specialist audience, it can still prove stimulating to the expert.

Contents: From Descriptive to Molecular
Embryology. How Genes Direct the Synthesis
of Specific Proteins. How Eggs and Embryos
Are Made. Gametogenesis and Maturation:
The Formation of Eggs and Spermatozoa.
Fertilization: How the Sleeping Egg Awakes.
Egg Cleavage: A Story of Cell Division.
Chemical Embryology of Invertebrate Eggs.
Chemical Embryology of Vertebrate Eggs.
Biochemical Interactions between the
Nucleus and the Cytoplasm during Morpho-
genesis. How Cells Differentiate. Problems
for Today and Tomorrow.

Springer-Verlag
Berlin Heidelberg New York

München Johannesburg London Madrid
New Delhi Paris Rio de Janeiro Sydney
Tokyo Utrecht Wien

E. Bünning:
The Physiological Clock

Circadian Rhythms and Biological Chrono-
metry. Third revised edition
134 figures. XIII, 258 pages. 1973
(Heidelberg Science Library, Vol. 1)
DM 17,40; US $6.70
ISBN 3-540-90067-5
Distribution rights for U.K., Commonwealth,
and the Traditional British Market (excluding
Canada): English Universities Press Ltd.,
London

Prices are subject to change without notice

The physiological clock has acquired particular significance with the advent of inter-
continental air travel and space travel. This
book gives a detailed discussion of present-
day knowledge of the processes of basic to
this mechanism and the effects on the human
organism.

Contents: Endodiurnal Oscillations as the
Principle of Many Physiological Time-
Measuring Processes. — Periodicity Fade-
Out; Initiation by External Factors. —
Autonomy of Cells and Organs; Controlling
Systems. — Temperature Effects. — Light
Effects. — Attempts toward a Kinetic Ana-
lysis: Models. — Attempts toward a Bio-
chemical and Biophysical Analysis. — Adjust-
ment to Diurnal Cycles in the Environment. —
Use of the Clock in Direction Finding. —
Relations between Circadian, Tidal, and
Lunar Rhythms. — Control of Diurnal Fluc-
tuations in Responsiveness to External
Factors. — Use of the Clock for Day-Length
Measurement. — Pathological Phenomena.

Springer-Verlag
Berlin Heidelberg New York

München Johannesburg London Madrid
New Delhi Paris Rio de Janeiro Sydney
Tokyo Utrecht Wien